AnimalWays

Butterflies

AnimalWays

Butterflies

GLORIA G. SCHLAEPFER

Marshall Cavendish
Benchmark
New York

Aspecial thank you to Jan Meerman for the lengthy interview he gave me and for introducing me to the wonders of tropical butterflies. And thank you to Dr. Dan Wharton, director of the Central Park Wildlife Center, for his expert reading of this manuscript.

Marshall Cavendish Benchmark
99 White Plains Road
Tarrytown, NY 10591
www.marshallcavendish.us

Library of Congress Cataloging-in-Publication Data
Schlaepfer, Gloria G.
Butterflies / by Gloria G. Schlaepfer.
p. cm. — (Animalways)
Includes bibliographical references and index.
ISBN 0-7614-1745-1
1. Butterflies—Juvenile literature. I. Title. II. Series: Animalways.

QL544.2.S386 2004
595.78'9—dc22

Photo Research by Candlepants Incorporated

Cover Photo: Minden Pictures/Tim Fitzharris

The photographs in this book are used by permission and through the courtesy of:
Peter Arnold, Inc.: Werner H. Muller, 2; Gunter Ziesler, 9; John R. MacGregor, 11; T. Da Chuna/BIOS, 12; Hans Pfletschinger, 15, 34, 35, 37, 63; Luberon/BIOS, 23; S. J. Krasemann, 29; M & C Photography, 33 (bottom); Prevot/BIOS, 40, 58; Kevin Schafer, 43; Manfred Kage, 45; G. Mermet/BIOS, 46; J. Y. Gropas/BIOS, 51; Darlyne A. Murawski, 59, 60, 65; Lior Rubin, 61; Luiz C. Marigo, 68, 87; Carl R. Sams II, 71 (left); David Cavagnard, 73; Kevin Schafer, 74, back cover; Manfred Danegger, 75; Don Riepe, 81; *Corbis*: Robbie Jack, 14; Paul Almasy, 17; Tom Bean, 20; Steve Kaufman, 33 (top), 83; George D. Lepp, 41; Michael & Patricia Fogden, 54; Tecmap Corporation/Eric Curry, 71 (right); William Manning, 84; Gary W. Carter, 86; Danny Lehman, 94; Roman Soumar, 98; Martin Rogers, 100; *Bruce Coleman, Inc.*: John Shaw, 79; *Photo Researchers, Inc.*: A. H. Rider, 89; *Minden Pictures*: Frans Lanting, 95, 97.

Printed in China

1 3 5 6 4 2

Contents

Animal Kingdom

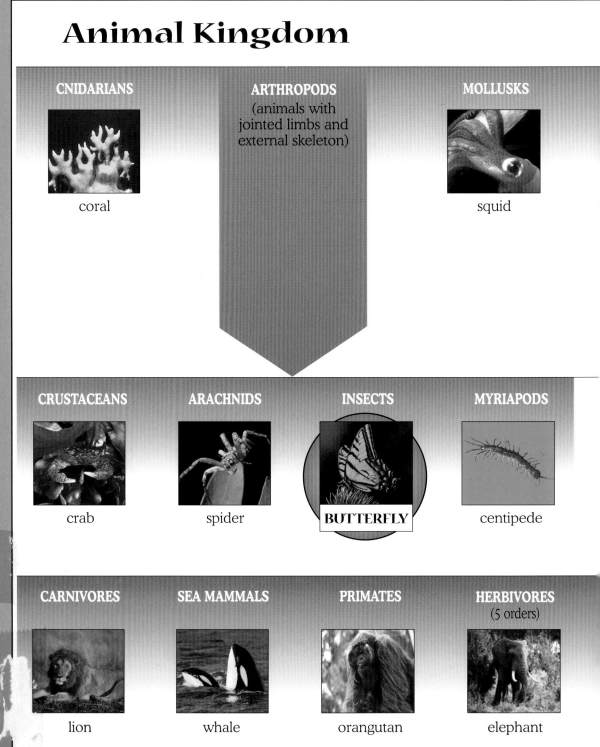

CNIDARIANS

coral

ARTHROPODS
(animals with jointed limbs and external skeleton)

MOLLUSKS

squid

CRUSTACEANS

crab

ARACHNIDS

spider

INSECTS

BUTTERFLY

MYRIAPODS

centipede

CARNIVORES

lion

SEA MAMMALS

whale

PRIMATES

orangutan

HERBIVORES
(5 orders)

elephant

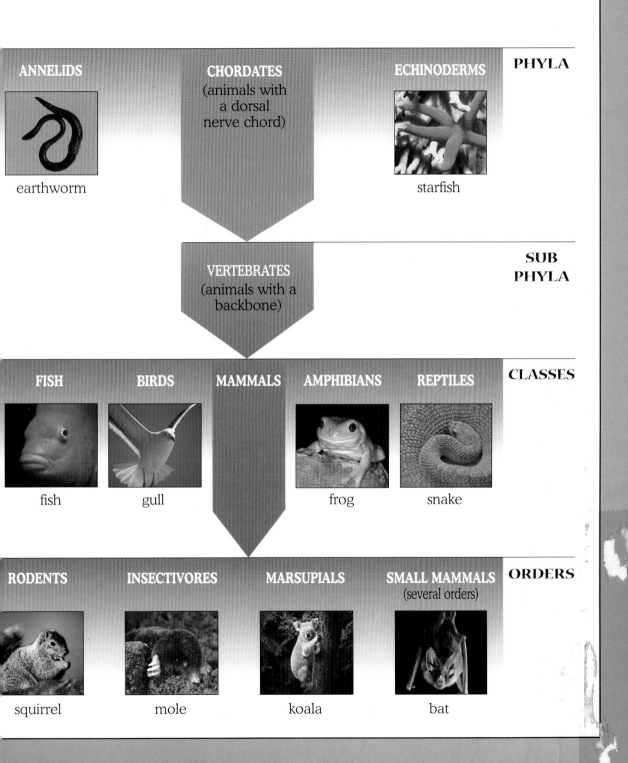

PHYLA

ANNELIDS

earthworm

CHORDATES
(animals with
a dorsal
nerve chord)

ECHINODERMS

starfish

**SUB
PHYLA**

VERTEBRATES
(animals with a
backbone)

CLASSES

FISH

fish

BIRDS

gull

MAMMALS

AMPHIBIANS

frog

REPTILES

snake

ORDERS

RODENTS

squirrel

INSECTIVORES

mole

MARSUPIALS

koala

SMALL MAMMALS
(several orders)

bat

1

Beautiful Butterflies

Nature's long-awaited spring season never grows old. Violets and columbines, colorful wildflowers, sway gently as they welcome an array of lovely and delicate butterflies. Fiery-orange and black painted ladies flutter gracefully, stopping to sip nectar at one flower after another. Checkered skippers, no bigger than the end of a pinkie finger, dart about the flowering fields. And above, two cabbage whites court and dance together. Beautiful and graceful, butterflies lift our spirits with their loveliness and lyric flight.

But butterflies are more than objects of beauty. They play an active role in nature's web of life. Like bees, butterflies depend on flowers for nectar, and plants depend on the insects for pollination.

THE BLUE MORPHO OPENS ITS BRILLIANT METALLIC
BLUE WINGS AND BASKS IN THE SUNSHINE.

As butterflies sip a flower's nectar, pollen collects on their feet and bodies and is carried to the next flower. In that way, butterflies, bees, and other animals pollinate the flowers, so the plants can develop seeds.

Besides pollination, butterflies in all phases of their life cycle are an important part of nature's food chain. They are vital food for birds, reptiles, mammals, and other insects.

Scaled Wings

Butterflies, together with moths, make up a large order or group of insects called Lepidoptera, which means scaly wings. The word Lepidoptera comes from the Greek words *lepis* for scale and *ptera*, meaning wing. All lepidoptera have tiny scales on their bodies and wings that overlap like shingles on a house. The scales give the wings their often-vibrant colors and unique patterns. There are about 170,000 known species of lepidoptera. More than 140,000 are moths, while only 18,500 are butterflies.

Size

With so many species, butterflies vary greatly in color, wing size, and shape. The tiniest butterfly, the pygmy blue, is less than three-fourths of an inch (19 mm) wide and could easily sit on the tip of your nose. In contrast, the Queen Alexandra's birdwing, the largest butterfly in the world, has a wingspan of 5 to 11 inches (127–279 mm), greater than some birds.

Moth or Butterfly?

No one characteristic separates butterflies from moths. Both go through four stages in their life cycles. Starting at the egg stage, they hatch into caterpillars, which feed greedily on plants before entering the pupa or chrysalis stage. From there, they emerge as flying adults, ready to feed on nectar, breed, and start the next generation of butterflies and moths.

Most butterflies are diurnal, or active during the day, when there is sunshine. A few species in rainforests are crepuscular; that is, they stir at dawn or dusk. In contrast, most moths are night-flyers or nocturnal insects.

Butterflies and moths differ in other ways. Butterflies have

BUTTERFLIES, LIKE THIS BLACK SWALLOWTAIL, HAVE LONG BODIES AND THIN ANTENNAE THAT END IN A KNOB.

long, thin antennae that end in a small knob. The antennae of moths may be thin, feathery, or comblike, but they almost never end in a knob.

Most moths have thick bodies. Often, the colors are dull brown, which may serve to camouflage them. They may be as tiny as the clothes moth or as large and strikingly beautiful as the African moon moth.

Moths have a tiny hook or bristle that links the forewings and hindwings together. Linked, the moth's wings can fold down over its back or wrap around its body. Moths also hold their wings straight out to the side, like the wings of an airplane.

Butterfly wings do not have a hook. When resting or feeding, the insect holds its wings upright over its body. When butterflies bask in the sun, their wings open flat to catch the sun's warmth.

A CLOSE-UP OF A BUTTERFLY'S WING SHOWS THE SUPPORTING VEINS AND THE THOUSANDS OF TINY SCALES.

The wings of butterflies are often larger, more colorful, and more dramatically marked than moth wings. And butterflies generally have longer, thinner, less shaggy bodies. Some skippers, though, have heavy, hairy bodies. For the most part, the above descriptions help to distinguish a butterfly from a moth.

What's in a Name

Poets have called butterflies winged flowers, flutterflies, and flying gems. So how did this lovely creature get the name butterfly? The name first appeared in the Middle Ages as *buter-coleur flye*, probably named for the common yellow brimstone, a deep buttery-colored butterfly. Over time, the name changed to *buterflye* and then *butterfly*.

Playful Names

Have you noticed how many times we use the word butterfly to describe other objects and actions? For example, there is the butterfly stroke in swimming. The swimmer's arms come forward in circular motions in such a way that they resemble the shape of butterfly wings.

We say we have butterflies in our stomach when we get nervous, and our belly feels queasy. Small, brightly colored butterfly fishes display a darting behavior similar to some butterflies. There is a butterfly chair, butterfly value, butterfly knot, butterfly bandage, and a butterfly shell. Butterfly shrimp are slit open and flattened to resemble butterfly wings. There are butterfly flowers and a butterfly bush. The bright orange flowers of the bush attract swarms of butterflies in summer, giving the plant its name.

Sometimes, the name butterfly suggests fragility as in the

SOPRANO LIPING ZHANG
PORTRAYS CHO CHO SAN
IN THE TRAGIC OPERA
MADAMA BUTTERFLY. HERE
SHE SINGS OF HER LOVE FOR
PINKERTON, AN AMERICAN
NAVAL OFFICER.

tragic opera *Madama Butterfly* by Giacomo Puccini. The heroine *Cho Cho San* (*cho cho* is Japanese for butterfly) is a beautiful and delicate young Japanese woman who falls in love and marries an American naval officer. His deception and betrayal lead to her tragic death.

Butterflies around the World

Butterflies can be found almost everywhere in the world, with the exception of Antarctica. They occur in temperate climates, in the cold arctic within six degrees of the North Pole, and on mountains—more than 18,000 feet (5,500 m) high. They are most abundant in the tropics. Lepidopterists, or scientists who study butterflies, group them together according to their biological similarity and place them into six geographical regions.

The *Palearctic Region* is the largest. It stretches across the Northern Hemisphere from western Europe to Asia all the way to the Pacific Ocean. From the Arctic, the region extends south into the Sahara Desert of North Africa. Overall, the climate of this region is mainly temperate and seasonal—warm summers and cold winters. Some areas, as the name suggests, are very cold. Other locations are subtropical; that is, warmer and wetter than the temperate lands. Two of the better-known butterfly species of this region include the common blue and the Old World swallowtail. The swallowtail is a large butterfly with a bold pattern of black and yellow, marked by red eyespots on each hindwing.

The *Nearctic Region* is temperate in climate also. It does, however, cover arctic Canada and Alaska as well subtropical

THE BOLDLY COLORED OLD WORLD SWALLOWTAIL IS FOUND THROUGHOUT THE PALEARCTIC REGION AND IN PARTS OF THE NEARCTIC REGION.

Florida and California. About 700 butterfly species inhabit the region. The most familiar is the monarch, noted for its long annual migration south for the winter.

The *Neotropical Region* extends from Mexico all the way to the tip of South America and contains many different habitats and climates. Its tropical rainforests hold the richest butterfly populations in the world. In Brazil's forests alone, there are over 2,000 species. The fast-flying beautiful blue morpho and the jewel-like Hewitson's blue hairstreak occur in the tropical forests.

Equally rich in butterflies are the *Indo-Malaysian* and *Australian Regions*. These include the areas from India and Pakistan to New Zealand and Australia. The climate is mostly tropical. Rice fields, rainforest, swamps, and mountains typify the diverse habitats. Found throughout Southeast Asia, the birdwing butterflies have wingspans of up to 11 inches (28 cm), making them the biggest and most exquisite butterflies in the world.

The *Afrotropical* or *Ethiopian Region* claims more than 2,500 butterfly species. Diverse in habitats—rainforest, grasslands, and savannas—the region covers all of Africa south of the Sahara. The African giant swallowtail, with its characteristic orange and black patterning, is the largest butterfly in Africa. It inhabits tropical areas, as does the tailless black and yellow citrus swallowtail.

Butterfly as Symbol in Religion and Myth

For people in the ancient world, the transformation of a fat caterpillar into a beautiful butterfly must have seemed miraculous. In early cultures, religions, art, and myths, butterflies became symbols of immortality, fleeting beauty, and freedom.

The butterfly as a symbol of immortality or the deathlessness of the human soul emerged in the neolithic or late Stone Age. The Butterfly Goddess, also called the goddess of rebirth, surfaced around 5000 B.C.E. Simple drawings show her holding double axe blades at her shoulders, representing butterfly wings. The goddess also appeared symbolically in the form of double ax blades painted on vases and stone coffins.

The ancient Greeks (1200–224 B.C.E.) believed in eternal life through reincarnation or rebirth of the soul in a new body. The butterfly became a symbol for the birth and death of the human soul. Aristotle, the Greek philosopher and scientist, made a connection between immortality and butterflies in his book, *Historia Animalium* (History of Animals), written in 344 B.C.E. In it, he classified and named many animals, choosing the name Psyche for butterflies. Psyche also means soul, mind, or life in Greek.

In Greek mythology, Psyche is a young princess whose tasks and sorrows stand for the struggles of the human soul. In her mythological story, Psyche's beauty arouses the jealousy of the goddess Aphrodite. She orders Eros (Cupid) to make Psyche fall

PSYCHE RIDES A CAMEL IN THIS STONE WALL SCULPTURE, CIRCA FIRST CENTURY B.C.E.– THIRD CENTURY C.E.

in love with a monster. Instead, Eros falls in love with Psyche. He tells her she must not see his face. One night, she learns his identity, and Eros vanishes. Grieving, Psyche asks Aphrodite for help, but the goddess demands three difficult tasks of Psyche. She dies trying to complete the last one. A heartbroken Eros goes to Zeus, the father of the gods, and asks him to bring Psyche back to life. Zeus grants the wish and reunites the couple. Zeus also gives Psyche immortal life. She is often portrayed in Greek sculpture as a beautiful young woman with butterfly wings.

Goddesses in Mesoamerica

In the ancient Mayan and Aztec cultures of Mexico and Central America, the people closely observed all the animals around them. With thousands of butterflies in Mexico and Central America, it is not surprising that butterflies captivated the interest of these early Middle American peoples.

Butterflies represented fire, death, soul, warriors, and even hummingbirds. Two butterfly goddesses, Xochiquetzal and Itzpapalotl, played an important part in the religion and the everyday life of the people.

Xochiquetzal, or beautiful flower, was the goddess of love, flowers, vegetation, and fire. The goddess represented the common western tiger swallowtail, the Xochiquetzal butterfly. Greatly respected, Xochiquetzal was the protector of artists and the mother of *Quetzalcoatl*, the god of Life.

Itzpapalotl, the obsidian butterfly goddess of four knives, was the mother goddess of the *Chichimec* people who lived in Mexico in the twelfth and thirteenth centuries C.E. Her name comes from the obsidian butterfly, which has four triangular patterns on its wings. The patterns look like knife blades.

Itzpapalotl, depicted with butterfly wings and big claws, was a strong and fierce goddess.

In ancient Mexico, both butterflies and fire represented transformation. Their symbols appear together on the outer edges of the Aztec calendar. In other pre-Columbian art works, butterfly forms adorn stone sculpture and ceramic pieces. The artists portrayed the insects realistically as well as in abstract form.

American Southwest

Farther north, butterflies figure importantly in Native American rituals and myths. Among the Hopi people, one clan uses the totem or emblem of the butterfly for its name. Butterfly designs decorate traditional pottery and woven baskets.

In their rituals, three of the many Hopi kachinas represent the butterfly's spirit: Poli Mana, butterfly girl; Poli Taka, butterfly man; and Poli Sio Hemis, a Zuni butterfly kachina. Kachinas are supernatural beings that act as messengers between the gods and the people.

Native American tribes gather in late summer to share cultural traditions and dances. The butterfly dance is most popular. In one version, the butterfly maiden with her feather fan dances and spreads the pollinating spirit of the butterfly over the earth and its people. It is an appeal for rain, good health, and long life for all living beings.

Japanese Mythology

Japan is a country rich in myths, legends, and folktales. Butterflies often appear in stories as the souls of departed humans. A favorite Japanese legend relates the story of a young couple who loved their garden as much as they did each other. After

they died in old age, their son continued to carefully tend the garden. The next spring, two butterflies emerged and visited the garden each day. One night the son dreamt his parents returned and walked around the flowers. Suddenly, they became butterflies. The next morning, the son saw the two butterflies in the garden, and he believed they were the souls of his parents who came back to enjoy their garden again.

Designs, Fantasy, and Art

Butterflies appeal to us because they are so beautiful. For centuries, artists used the images of the insects, sometimes in combination with flowers and birds, to produce paintings and to decorate jewelry, clothing, books, and everyday objects. The images brought charm and delicacy to popular and fashionable items.

During the late Middle Ages, wealthy people cherished beautifully adorned manuscripts and daily prayer books. The artisan monks worked with vivid inks and gold leaf to enrich their drawings. Often, the colorful drawings included butterflies, drawn in a naturalistic and pleasing style.

To brighten their clothing and, later, to identify warriors in battle, Japanese nobility in the eleventh century created family crests, or emblems. Butterflies became popular subjects for the highly stylized and symmetrical designs on the crests.

In the contemporary world of fashion, internationally recognized designer Hanae Mori utilizes butterfly images in many of her exquisite creations. Embroidered butterflies lavishly color the rich silk and satin gowns, robes, and wall hangings. She says her butterfly motif is a symbol of hope, fragility, and beauty.

Watercolor artist Cicely Mary Barker found inspiration for her illustrations in the radiant and brilliant colors of butterfly wings. In her *Flower Fairy* books, each flower fairy has a pair of butterfly-like wings and wears a costume that mimics a flower.

Butterflies continue to inspire and capture the imagination of other artists working with paint, glass, gold, and textiles. Butterflies capture our interest as well. Yet, just as we begin to enjoy and value them, they are disappearing from our gardens and the wild places in the world. Sadly, many butterfly species have already become extinct. The more we learn about butterflies, their behavior, and needs, the more we may find ways to conserve them.

2

A Look Back in Time

At first glance, the ancient forest of towering trees and prickly-leafed cycads seems peaceful as the animals go about their daily lives. Duck-billed hadrosaurs crisscross through the forest as they wind their way to their marshy feeding grounds. Giant dragonflies hover overhead like helicopters, hoping to catch a juicy beetle, while brown-winged butterflies cluster together in a thicket of flowers.

A tiny mammal peers out from its burrow and watches. Silently, it moves quickly towards the butterflies. Snap! It grabs one in its sharp teeth and scurries back to its home. Predators lurk everywhere in the Cretaceous world.

THIS FOSSILIZED BUTTERFLY, *LETHE CORBIERI*, FROM THE OLIGOCENE PERIOD, WAS FOUND IN FRANCE.

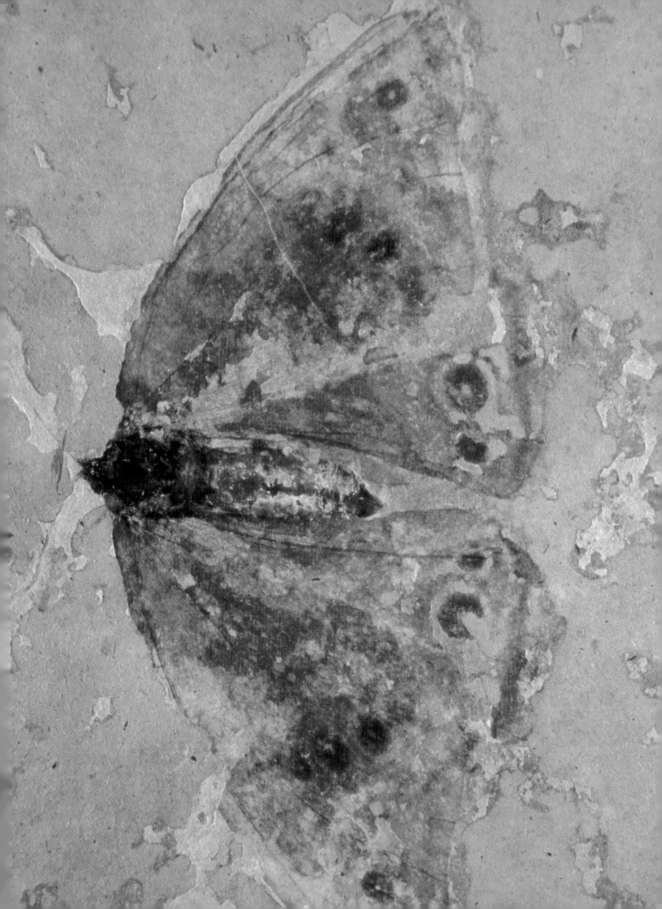

For the next 75 million years, butterflies evolved and adapted to new climates, animals, and plants. In doing so, they found many ways to protect themselves. Butterflies are dramatically successful insects.

Insect Ancestry

Butterflies and moths make up a small number of the more than two million insects on earth. Ants, silverfish, cockroaches, bees, flies, grasshoppers, mosquitoes, and many not yet named are all part of this large, diverse group of animals called insects.

It took millions and millions of years for insects to evolve to their present life forms. Changes occurred continuously in a series of big leaps forward, followed by long pauses where nothing seemed to happen. Some geological periods produced an explosion of new insects. At the same time, other species died out. Other periods brought variations in mouthparts, the origin of wings, and the development of metamorphosis, or

Evolution of Insects

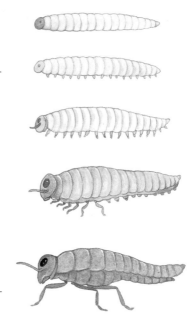

INSECTS EVOLVED SLOWLY FROM SIMPLE, SEGMENTED, WORMLIKE ANIMALS. OVER EONS, THESE WINGLESS CREATURES DEVELOPED FEET ON EACH SEGMENT. THEN, AS THE SEGMENTS SEPARATED, THEY FORMED THE HEAD, THORAX, AND ABDOMEN. ANTENNAE, EYES, MOUTH-PARTS, WINGS, AND TRUE LEGS APPEARED. THE FINAL RESULT IS THE MODERN INSECT.

the complete change from one stage to the next in the life of an organism.

The primitive-looking wingless silverfish gave scientists important clues to the evolution of all insects. Entomologists, scientists who study insects, believe the ancestor of insects looked like a silverfish. It had a segmented wormlike body with a pair of feet on each segment. Over millions of years, the feet lengthened to form legs that provided more mobility. The segments gradually merged into three parts to form the head, thorax, and abdomen. Millions of changes to this basic arrangement led to the phenomenal diversity of insects.

The oldest insect fossils date from the early Carboniferous period, about 300 million years ago. The insects had fully developed wings and the three-part bodies. Those advanced features suggested to entomologists that insects had been evolving for a long time.

The primitive winged insects probably looked like dragonflies do today. Their four large glassy-looking wings extend straight out from their bodies, like the wings of an airplane. The wings do not fold over their backs as in beetles and moths. But despite their primitive wings, dragonflies are champion flyers and dangerous predators.

By the mid-Tertiary period—26 to 40 million years ago—all the orders of modern insects had come into existence.

Geological Time

Scientists divide the earth's long history into units called eras— Precambrian, Paleozoic, Mesozoic, and Cenozoic. The eras are subdivided into periods, and some periods into epochs. Each division represents the changes that occurred in life forms as found in fossils. Think of geological time as a calendar with

THE GEOLOGICAL TIME SCALE

Era	Period	Epoch
Cenozoic (65 million years ago–present)	**Quaternary** (1.8 million years ago–present)	**Holocene** (8,000 years ago–present)
		Pleistocene (1.8 million–8,000 years ago)
	Tertiary (65–1.8 million years ago)	**Pliocene** (5.3–1.8 million years ago)
		Miocene (23.8–5.3 million years ago)
		Oligocene (33.7–23.8 million years ago)
		Eocene (55–33.7 million years ago)
		Paleocene (65–55.5 million years ago)
Mesozoic (248–65 million years ago)	**Cretaceous** (145–65 million years ago)	
	Jurassic (213–145 million years ago)	
	Triassic (248–213 million years ago)	
	Permian (286–248 million years ago)	
Paleozoic (544–248 million years ago)	**Carboniferous** (360–286 million years ago)	
	Devonian (410–360 million years ago)	
	Silurian (440–410 million years ago)	
	Ordovician (505–440 million years ago)	
	Cambrian (544–505 million years ago)	
Precambrian (Beginning of earth about 4.5 billion years ago– 544 million years ago)		

the building up of days into weeks, weeks into months, years, centuries, and, finally millennia.

Fossilized Butterflies

Scientists found the first fossilized butterflies in Cretaceous rock from the Mesozoic era, which was 65 to 145 million years ago. Butterfly fossils, however, are scarce. Unlike beetles and dragonflies, the soft bodies and delicate wings of butterflies decay before they can be preserved and hardened as fossils in rock. Some butterflies, though, have been preserved in amber. Fewer than fifty butterfly fossils have been found so far, and most date from a later time—the Eocene in the Tertiary period.

The large gaps and scanty fossil record do not mean butterflies appeared spontaneously on Earth. Entomologists looked at the fossil evidence of both butterflies and other insects in order to piece together the evolutionary puzzle. The scientists concluded that by the end of the Mesozoic era butterflies had developed most of their modern features. In other words, modern swallowtail butterflies closely resemble 50-million-year-old butterfly fossils. Entomologists also point out that flowering plants (hosts to butterflies) evolved during the same geological periods.

Insects Take to the Air

The development of wings is an insect success story. Wings enabled the early insects to expand their habitats by moving from land to air. They could explore farther to find food or mates and fly to escape from predators.

Scientists have speculated about the evolution of wings in insects. One theory suggests that outgrowths, or little flattened flaps, arose from the thorax or chest of primitive insects. The flaps extended sideways and allowed the early insects to leap or glide farther. Other scientists theorize that wings originated from tracheal gills, air-carrying tubes found in insects living near water. With the aid of the wind, the primitive wings carried the insects to new habitats.

As wings grew in length, insects could control the direction of their flight. And as the muscles developed in the chest, the insects could flap their wings and fly greater distances. Insects became the masters of the air before the pterosaurs, bats, or birds.

Eyes of Many Lenses

Along with the ability to fly, primitive insects evolved better eyesight. Some insects have simple eyes called ocelli. Each ocellus contains one large lens with a layer of many light-sensitive elements behind it. With simple eyes, insects react to changes in light but cannot see images. It may be that they rely on their sense of hearing or smell more than their sight.

Most insects, such as butterflies, flies, and wasps, have two large compound eyes made up of light-sensitive units called ommatidia. They quickly detect any movement or change around them, an advantage to flying insects. Compound eyes do not have the ability to focus, so clear vision is limited to a yard (0.9 m). Beyond that, images appear as a blur.

Body Transformation—Metamorphosis

In addition to wings, metamorphosis was a major evolutionary development in insects. It probably evolved as winged adults took advantage of new environments, separate from their larvae. Gradually, the mouthparts and limbs of each changed so an insect's adult and larva forms became distinctly different. For

most insects, an intermediate pupal stage evolved. It tied together the forms and structure of larva and adult.

Pathways to Adulthood

When an insect egg hatches, it follows one of three paths. The first or simple path occurs in a few primitive insects, such as silverfish. After they hatch, the juvenile silverfish look exactly like adults except smaller. As they grow larger, they molt, or shed, their old skins until they are adults.

The second path, incomplete metamorphosis, occurs in insects such as dragonflies, roaches, and cicadas. They go through three phases: egg, nymph, and adult. Among the different insects, the nymph stage varies greatly. For example, the nymphs of grasshoppers look and behave as adults except for being wingless. As the nymph grows and molts, its wings appear and become larger with each molt.

In contrast, the wingless nymphs of dragonflies live in water and breathe with gills. At the end of this phase, the nymph crawls out of the water and onto a plant or rock. Then it sheds its shell for the last time and becomes an adult dragonfly.

Complete metamorphosis is the third path used by most

insects, including butterflies. Metamorphosis occurs in four stages: egg, larva, pupa, and adult. The wormlike larvae, or caterpillars, of butterflies live in different places than adults. They also have chewing mouthparts and eat different foods. Once the larva stops growing, it enters the pupa or resting stage. There the body of the larva is broken down and completely reorganized to form the tissues, wings, and organs of the adult butterfly.

Complete metamorphosis allows larvae and adults to specialize and perform different roles. The outcome is the most successful evolutionary strategy for survival of an insect species.

Bugs by Another Name

When is a bug a bug? Many people call any creepy crawly creature a bug. They could mean a caterpillar, pill bug, roach, centipede, and even the flu bug. Yet, entomologists gently remind us that the word bug refers only to insects in the order Hemiptera. Stink bugs and water striders are examples of true bugs.

To give order to the identification and classification of all organisms, the Swedish scientist Carolus Linnaeus (1707–1778) developed the scientific method of nomenclature, or naming. In it, each organism has a name with two parts. The first part is the genus, or group, in which all organisms are classified based on some shared characteristics. The second part of the name is the species, or kind. Organisms with the same species name are always very similar.

In addition, organisms are part of a large system of classification made up of seven major groups: kingdom, phylum, class, order, family, genus, and species. The kingdom is the largest, while species is the smallest. For example, butterflies belong to the Animal kingdom, phylum Arthropoda, class Insecta, and order Lepidoptera.

In the phylum Arthropoda, the animals have six or more pairs of jointed legs and an external skeleton or hard outer shell that covers their segmented bodies. Within the phylum Arthropoda, there are nine separate classes. The animals in each class have distinctive features that separate them from the other classes. The most familiar classes are the millipedes, the arachnids (spiders), the crustaceans (crabs and pill bugs), the centipedes, and the insects.

Class Insecta

The largest numbers of arthropods are in the class Insecta. The two million insect species are magnificently diverse. By looking at the structure of their wings, mouthparts, and means of reproduction, scientists place them into smaller groups called orders. For instance, adult butterflies and moths have siphoning mouthparts shaped like coiled tubes, and scaly wings, so they belong to the order Lepidoptera.

The orders break down further into suborders, superfamilies, families, genera, and species. With each division, the insects have more features in common. Butterflies belong to the suborder Rhopalocera, meaning those with clubbed antennae. Moths reside in the suborder Heterocera.

Butterfly Classification: Latin Spoken Here

Many taxonomists, scientists who classify organisms, recognize the division of butterflies into the superfamily Papilionoidea (true butterflies) and the superfamily Hesperioidea for skippers. Some taxonomists also place true butterflies into four very large families: Papilionidae, Pieridae, Lycaenidae, and Nymphalidae. Because they are large and diverse, they are often divided into subfamilies.

Within each family, an organism has its specific Latin name

of genus and species. All the species in a genus are related, but each species is unique to itself. To illustrate, both the giant swallowtail and tiger swallowtail butterflies have striking yellow and black markings. They inhabit North America, belong to the family Papilionidae and the genus *Papilio*. But based on dissimilarities in all stages of their life cycles, they are separate species. The classification of the swallowtail butterflies looks like this:

Common name: Giant swallowtail	**Common name:** Tiger swallowtail
Kingdom: Animalia	**Kingdom**: Animalia
Phylum: Arthropoda	**Phylum**: Arthropoda
Class: Insecta	**Class**: Insecta
Order: Lepidoptera	**Order**: Lepidoptera
Suborder: Rhopalocera	**Suborder**: Rhopalocera
Family: Papilionidae	**Family**: Papilionidae
Genus: *Papilio*	**Genus**: *Papilio*
Species: *cresphontes*	**Species**: *glaucus*

The Families of True Butterflies

Family Papilionidae—Swallowtails. Many butterflies in this family have tail-like projections on their hindwings that look like the tails of swallows. This family also includes the Queen Alexandra's birdwing, found in Southeast Asia, the biggest and most beautiful butterfly in the world. The Papilionids are slow-wandering tropical butterflies.

Family Pieridae—Whites, Sulphurs, and Orange Tips. These small- to medium-sized butterflies have white, yellow, and orange wing colors, although individuals of the same species may vary in pattern and color. Found worldwide, they frequent open sunny places such as meadows and gardens. The caterpillar

THIS YELLOW BUTTERFLY'S BLACK
STRIPES AND TAILED WINGS IDENTIFY
IT AS A TIGER SWALLOWTAIL.

A CLOUDED SULPHUR BUTTERFLY
CLINGS TO A DEW-LADEN PLANT STEM.

of the cabbage white butterfly is considered a pest, as it can be quite destructive to cabbages and related plants.

Family Lycaenidae—Gossamer-wings. One-third of all butterflies belong to this large, diverse family. The four subfamilies—coppers, metalmarks, blues, and hairstreaks—are distinctive, small, and dazzlingly colored. These butterflies are found throughout the world. Males and females may differ in color, and the undersides of the wings usually vary from the upper. The hairstreaks and blues may have one or two eyespots on their hindwings.

Family Nymphalidae—Brush-footed. More than 5,000 species comprise this diverse family, including the morphos, monarchs, fritillaries, and admirals. This family's common name, brush-footed, refers to the butterfly's underdeveloped pair of front legs, which are too short for walking. These medium-sized butterflies are good flyers, and several migrate long distances.

Unusual Families: Skippers, Moth Butterflies, Butterfly Moths

Family Hesperiidae—Skippers. Known worldwide as skippers, these butterflies have large heads and heavy bodies, but often lack clubbed antennae. They get their name from their characteristic flying behavior of skipping from flower to flower. Many are small- to medium-sized insects with orange to brown colors.

Family Castniidae—Moth Butterflies. This family of medium to large diurnal moth butterflies has clubbed antennae and unusually striking patterned wings.

Family Hedylidae—Butterfly Moths. These butterfly moths, as they are sometimes called, are both nocturnal and diurnal. They do not have the clubbed antennae of butterflies. When at rest, they spread their wings open, as moths do, and raise them slightly.

Butterflies made many evolutionary changes and adaptations throughout geologic time. Their diversity and ability to live in most climates have made them successful insects. And they delight us with their variety of colors, shapes, and sizes.

THE LARGE SIZE AND LACK OF PATTERNING ON ITS WINGS DISTINGUISHES THE LARGE SKIPPER FROM OTHER SKIPPER SPECIES.

3 Butterfly Bodies Inside and Out

> IN THE END WE WILL CONSERVE ONLY WHAT WE
> LOVE. WE LOVE ONLY WHAT WE UNDERSTAND. WE
> WILL UNDERSTAND ONLY WHAT WE ARE TAUGHT.
>
> —Senegalese ecologist Baba Dioum

The sun is still warm late in the afternoon when the fiery skipper flies to the lantana bush. The skipper's long proboscis uncoils, plunges down into a flower, and slowly sips the nectar. Realizing, perhaps, that the flower holds more, the skipper bends its head closer to the flower so the proboscis can reach the bottom. When satisfied, the skipper flies to another flower for another sweet drink.

COILED UP LIKE A SPRING, A BUTTERFLY'S
PROBOSCIS SITS UNDER THE HEAD.

An Adult Butterfly's Body

Transformed into a flying insect, clothed with flashy wings, clubbed antennae, and a coiled drinking tube, an adult butterfly looks nothing like its fat caterpillar.

Adult butterflies have the simple body plan found in all insects: head, thorax, and abdomen. Its skeleton, called an exoskeleton, is on the outside of its body. Made of a tough material called chitin, it is light in weight, strong, and wraps around the body to protect the insect like a suit of armor. We humans, in contrast, have an internal skeleton of bones.

Head. The butterfly's head—small and rounded in shape—has two enormous compound eyes. Between them sit the two long clubbed antennae.

An adult butterfly's mouth does not contain chewing or sucking parts. Instead, the jaws lock together to form the slender

Butterfly Exoskeleton

proboscis or hollow drinking tube. Coiled up like a spring, it sits under the head as part of a hollow bulblike cavity. When a butterfly's feet land on a flower, the proboscis immediately uncoils and extends forward. As muscles tighten, the air pressure inside the hollow cavity dips lower than the outside air pressure. That causes the nectar to move up the proboscis. A cap closes its end so the nectar does not leak out, and the sweet liquid flows into the esophagus.

Many butterflies have a very long proboscis that reaches into long-tubed flowers; others do not. The zebra swallowtail is one example. It coevolved with flowers that have shallow blooms, such as milkweeds, so it needs only a short proboscis to feed.

Thorax. The thorax or middle section of the body consists of three tightly joined segments with a pair of legs on each. Some butterflies have short forelegs, so they appear to have four legs instead of six. All the slender jointed legs are weak, and butterflies can walk only short distances.

Butterfly wings also reside in the thorax. In its middle segment are the front wings, while the last segment holds the large rear wings. Strong muscles power the two sets of wings.

Abdomen. The third part of the body, the long tapering abdomen, houses the organs for reproduction, digestion, and excretion. A female's abdomen is generally rounder because she carries hundreds of eggs. The abdomen consists of ten segments. On the first eight segments is a pair of spiracles, or breathing holes, through which oxygen replaces carbon dioxide, as our lungs do for us.

Caterpillar Bodies

Compared to the adult butterfly, caterpillars are simple creatures. Nevertheless they vary greatly in size, shape, and color patterns. They might be naked or covered with hairs, bristles, or spines. They can be green, red, striped, or polka-dotted. Their bodies, however, are soft, flexible, long tubes, divided into thirteen segments and ending in a small head.

The head contains the sense organs: short antennae and six pairs of simple light-sensitive eyes or ocelli. The caterpillar uses all of its senses to find its way and locate food. Large biting jaws chomp rhythmically through leaves and flowers.

Under its head are special glands that produce silk. Most caterpillars spin silk threads onto the leaves and branches of the host plant. In addition to giving the caterpillar an almost unshakable grip, the sticky threads hold the dangling caterpillar as it pupates. Adult butterflies do not spin silk.

THIS SPINY CATERPILLAR OF THE RED ADMIRAL FEEDS ON WEEDY STINGING NETTLES.

On the first three segments of the caterpillar's thorax is a pair of openings called spiracles, which allow for breathing. There are also three pairs of stubby, jointed walking legs that end in a grasping claw. Later, those legs become the legs of the adult butterfly.

The caterpillar's abdomen with its ten segments is clearly the largest part of its body. Eight segments also have a pair of spiracles. Five of the segments have a pair of fleshy gripping prolegs with many tiny hooks, or crochets. They grab the surface of a leaf or stem like sticky tape. When the caterpillar moves, it

A CLOSE-UP REVEALS THE CATERPILLAR'S FLESHY PROLEGS AS THEY CLASP THE PLANT STEM.

raises one pair of prolegs at a time. As one pair goes down, the next lifts up, and the caterpillar propels itself forward. The prolegs are not true legs, however, and are shed with the caterpillar's last molt.

Butterfly Wings and Scales

Unlike the wings of birds and bats, butterfly wings are not modified limbs. Butterfly wings grow out of the thorax and consist of a core of strong tubelike vessels. Lepidopterists call them veins. As no fluid or blood moves through them, they are not veins in the true sense. The veins, however, provide structure and strength to the wing membranes, like the framing supports of a building. A clear thin membrane stretches and covers the veins to form the wings. The patterns of the veins are unique to each species, so lepidopterists use the patterns as an important characteristic in identification and classification of butterflies.

Most of us, though, learn to recognize butterflies by the colorful patterns of their wings. The colors come from the thousands of tiny, slightly flattened, air-filled scales that overlap and cover the membranous wings like mosaic tiles.

The scales are very small. It takes about 500, placed side-by-side, to measure an inch (2.54 cm); that is 250,000 scales per square inch (6.5 cm)! Each scale has its own peg that attaches to the wing and holds it in place. Scales are soft and rub off like colored dust when touched.

Some butterflies—such as the tropical Esmeralda butterfly—have transparent wings. The Esmeralda's wings are clear except for a faint dusting of scales and an eye-catching pink patch and yellow-rimmed eyespot on the hind wing. Without scales, the brown veins of the wings and their edges are very prominent.

The striking colors on butterfly wings come either from

Butterfly Body

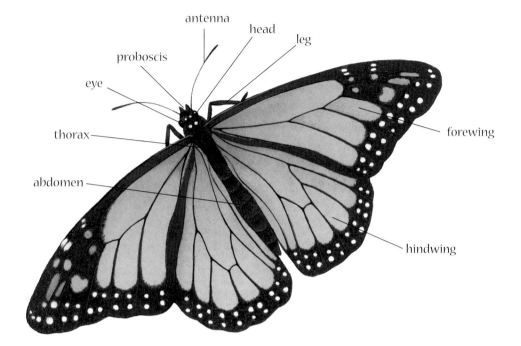

antenna
head
leg
proboscis
eye
thorax
abdomen
forewing
hindwing

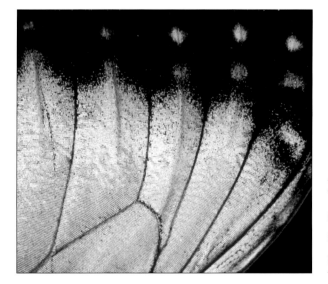

THE TINY OVERLAPPING
SCALES THAT COVER
BUTTERFLY WINGS LOOK
LIKE MOSAIC TILES.

pigments or the structure of the scales. Each scale has its own special color. Pigments are chemical compounds that absorb some wavelengths of multicolored light and reflect others. We see color from the reflected light that reaches our eyes. In the visual part of the color spectrum, or band of colors, we see the shortest wavelengths as violet and longest as red. Therefore, if a pigmented scale absorbs all the wavelengths except the longest one, we see the color as red. The colors depend also on the angle of the scales that reflect the light.

Two main pigments—pterins and melanins—account for most of the scale colors. Pterins create yellow, orange, red, and, sometimes, white colors. Melanins form the earth tones of dark yellow, tan, brown-red, brown, and black.

Nearly all the blues, most greens, and certainly all iridescence of scales come from structure, not pigment. It is the same effect as light striking a prism. As daylight strikes the elaborately ridged and grooved scale surface, the light rays bend and scatter. If the reflected light waves are short, the visible color is blue. Structural scales with some melanin create a brilliant iridescent or shimmering effect.

Colorful scales have important functions, too. They absorb or reflect sunlight to regulate body temperature. They attract potential mates, and they can camouflage to fool predators. If the scales rub off, the butterfly can still fly, but it may lose other functions.

Variable Wings

There is no one color, pattern, or size that describes all butterfly wings. They are extremely variable. The forewings can differ from the hindwings, and females may have larger wings than males.

In some species, the dorsal, or upper wing, surface is often

THE SUPPORTING VEINS, TINY SCALES, AND FRINGED EDGES ARE CLEARLY VISIBLE IN THIS CLOSE-UP OF THE COMMON MORPHO'S WINGS.

more colorful than the ventral, or undersurface. A good example is the common morpho butterfly. Its dorsal wing surface is a beautiful metallic blue, while the ventral side shows a brown background with a pattern of black and yellow-ringed eyespots. When its wings are upright or closed, only the undersurface is visible, and the morpho disappears into its resting place.

Butterfly Sense Organs

Butterflies may appear to fly around randomly, but they are actually intent on finding food and mates. To do so, they use all of their senses. Butterflies have fair eyesight, but a good sense of smell and taste. They probably do not hear sounds, although they respond to vibrations. Special sensory cells on the antennae and body pick up the vibrations.

The eyes are large and compound; that is, they have thousands of tiny light-sensitive lenses. Each lens, or ommatidium, sees only what is directly in front of it. But combined and set

THIS BUTTERFLY HAS DISTINCTLY BRIGHT EYESPOTS NEAR THE EDGE OF ITS WING.

closely together, the ommatidia create a picture for the butterfly to see in all directions without turning its head. Up close, the butterfly's eyes recognize some detail, but, in general, the eyes sense movement rather than providing a sharp image.

Butterflies see more colors than we see. Their vision extends from the red end of the spectrum to the near ultraviolet. Many flowers have a petal guide in their center (invisible to us) where nectar is found. Like an airport runway, the petal guide helps the butterfly zero in easily to find the food.

In many ways, butterflies depend on their vision, but their acute sense of smell is their greatest asset. Butterflies use their two antennae to search for food, to help them find their way about, to decide on which plants to lay their eggs, and greatly to help in attracting and identifying mates.

Males attract females by producing sex pheromones, or chemical scents, released through specific scales, or organs, called androconia. A female's antennae can detect the scents for distances of up to 1,000 feet (305 m). The powerful scents captivate and draw the females to the males.

While many insects taste with their antennae, butterflies taste with their six feet, or tarsi. They have an exceedingly keen sense of taste. As soon as a butterfly lands on a flower or plant, the sensitive taste receptors on the soles of the feet taste it. The butterfly learns if there is nectar for food, or if it is a good plant on which to lay its eggs.

Internal Organs

Circulation. Since the blood of butterflies does not transport oxygen as the red blood cells in our bodies do, it is greenish, yellowish, or colorless. Still, it flows to all parts of the body, carrying food and removing waste products from the cells.

There are no veins or arteries. Instead, a closed tube extends the length of the body just under the exoskeleton of the back. Blood enters the tube through small openings called ostia. Valves regulate the ostia by allowing blood to flow in but not out. The heart, located in the abdomen, pumps the blood and forces it along the tube to bathe all the body organs.

Caterpillar and Butterfly Organs

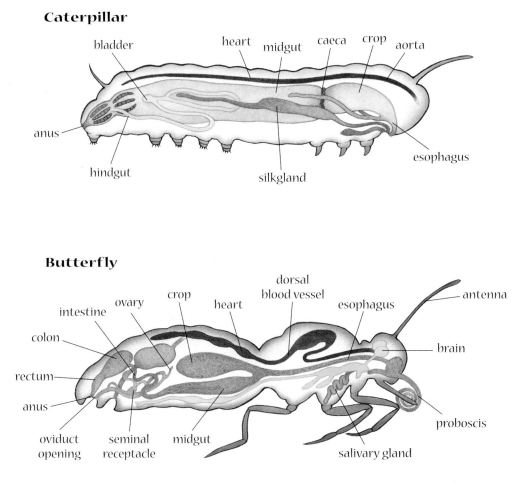

Caterpillar

Butterfly

Respiration. The respiratory system is relatively simple. It contains air-filled tubes or tracheae attached to the spiracles. In order to take in air, the abdomen pumps and provides the force needed to suck in air through some spiracles and push out air through others. The branched tracheae distribute oxygen to all the body cells and take away the carbon dioxide.

Digestive System. The simple digestive system consists of a long tube that stretches from the mouth to the anus. Food sucked up by the proboscis or chewed by the caterpillar's jaws enters the foregut. It continues to flow through the digestive tube to the crop, an enlarged storage area. From there, the food goes into the gizzard. Its muscular walls break up the food into small pieces before it moves into the midgut, or stomach. Most of the digestion takes place in the stomach with the help of enzymes such as protease and lipase. Nutrients from the digested food then pass into the blood. The undigested particles and wastes travel to the hindgut and leave the body through the anus.

Nervous System. Nerve cells that come together to form ganglion or nerve bundles make up the nervous system. The large ganglion in the head acts like a brain. It regulates most of the body's nervous system.

Connected to the brain are two long nerve cords that lie on the underside of the thorax and abdomen. The cords contain a series of connected ganglia. In each segment of the thorax and abdomen, the ganglia fuse together to form a mini-brain that directs the activity of that segment of the body.

Despite a relatively simple nervous system, butterflies use all of their senses and natural instincts to navigate through their world.

4 New Beginnings

THE CATERPILLAR WAS THE FIRST TO SPEAK.
"WHAT SIZE DO YOU WANT TO BE?" IT ASKED.
"OH, I'M NOT PARTICULAR AS TO SIZE," ALICE HASTILY REPLIED;
"ONLY ONE DOESN'T LIKE CHANGING SO OFTEN, YOU KNOW."
"I DON'T KNOW," SAID THE CATERPILLAR.

—Lewis Carroll, from *Alice's Adventures in Wonderland*, 1865

As the clouded sulphur butterfly crawls out of her pupal case, her wings fold loosely around her body. She grabs a near-by twig with her clawed feet and lets her crumpled wings hang down. The sulphur is free but cannot fly. She quickly pumps fluid into the veins of her wings until they expand completely. She waits patiently for them to dry.

A few hours later, a sense of urgency propels her into the air. Laden with eggs, she must find food and a mate within her short life span. The adult butterfly lives solely to survive and reproduce the next generation of its kind.

COURTING LACEWINGS PERCH TOGETHER ON A BRANCH.

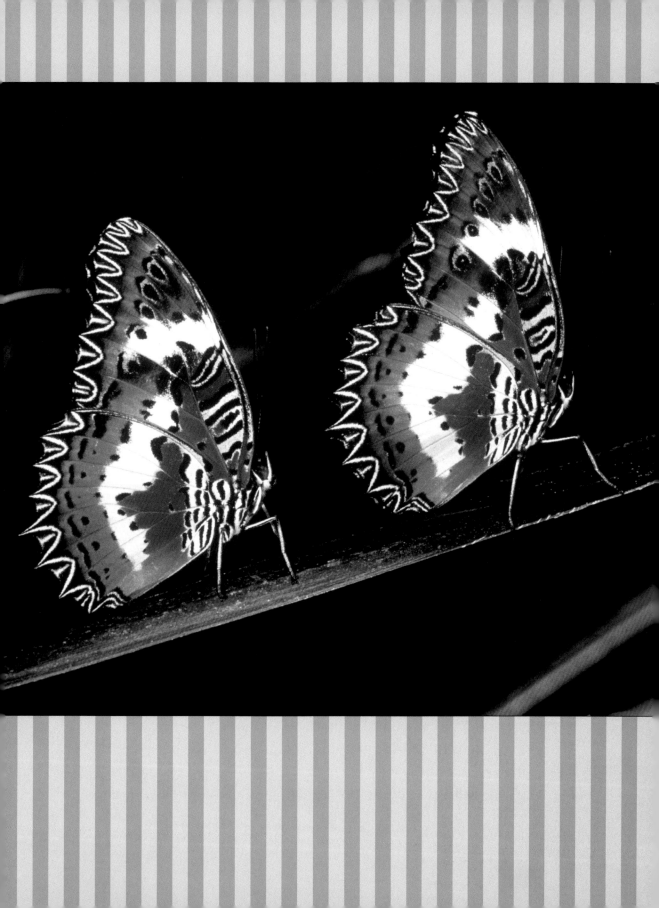

Courting Butterflies

The males actively search for females, using either the perch or patrol strategy. Perching males take a wait-and-look position from a plant, rock, log, or anywhere females visit regularly. The male is quite territorial; that is, he defends his space by chasing off other males, and even an occasional human. But if a female of his species enters his territory, the perching male pursues her.

A patrolling male, on the other hand, actively flies around looking for females. Once he recognizes a female of his species, he begins courting. The male has to entice her and convince her to mate with him.

At first, the vibrant wing colors and patterns attract the butterflies to each other, and they engage in an intricate, somewhat ritualistic, aerial dance. The male releases sex pheromones from special scales and organs called androconia. He flutters his wings and flies under and in front of the female, so the scents have a better chance of reaching her antennae.

A female that continues to fly signals a rejection of the male's wooing efforts. He may try again, wafting more pheromones in her direction. If she lands, the male may continue to flutter, touching her with his wings or antennae. When she accepts him, she holds her wings partially open, and he settles down at her side, continuing to spread his scent.

Mating

The butterflies curve their abdomens toward each other in a tail-to-tail position, and they copulate, or mate. It may take minutes or hours for the spermatophore to pass from the male to the female. It is a small capsule containing the sperm needed to fertilize the female's eggs. The spermatophore also has fats, salts, and other nutrients that provide some nourishment to the eggs.

After mating, the pair separate, and the male begins another search for females. But first, some males try to ensure that the female does not mate again, so his sperm alone can fertilize the eggs. He may spread a scent on the female so other males will ignore her. Parnassian butterfly males use another technique. A hard substance called a sphragis plugs the end of a female's abdomen. It acts like a chastity belt and effectively stops the female from mating again.

Butterfly Eggs

The pregnant female instinctively knows that she must oviposit, or lay, her eggs. It is not a simple matter, though. She has to find the right host plant that the caterpillars will eat. She smells the plant with her antennae and tastes it with her feet in order to judge the plant's condition and specific chemicals. This is particularly important for many species, such as the monarch caterpillar. It feeds only on plants in the milkweed family and will not recognize any other plant species as food.

Before the eggs are laid, the stored sperm of the male fertilizes them. The female then deposits her eggs on the most tender leaves, buds, or tendrils of the host plant. Some species place the eggs on the undersurface of a leaf, while others use the upper surface, sometimes hiding them in cracks or holes. Most females lay one egg at a time. Other species—Gillette checkerspots, mourningcloaks, and Milbert's tortoise shells—lay clusters of eggs. In contrast, the question mark butterfly lays a chain of eggs that dangles from the underside of a leaf, like pearl drops. A few species, whose caterpillars feed on grasses, simply scatter the eggs while flying over the host plants.

Each egg comes with waterproof glue that hardens to form

THE GROOVED EGGS OF A PIERID BUTTERFLY LOOK LIKE GOLDEN LANTERNS AS THEY
SIT IN PLACE ON A LEAF.

a protective case. Most butterflies can lay between 100 to 400
eggs. The Diana, however, lays more than 1,000 eggs. Predation
plays a large role in the number of eggs a female lays. The more
predation a species suffers, the more eggs it will lay to ensure
that some offspring survive to adulthood.

A New Generation

The egg is stuck in place. It is totally dependent on the female's
choice of a host plant, the site of deposit, and location in
the habitat. If it is lucky, the egg will hatch in four to ten days.
The warmer it is the more quickly an egg develops. There are

exceptions. A few species that overwinter in the egg stage can take as long as ten months to develop.

The tiny butterfly eggs come in a variety of shapes and colors. Examples include the green cone-shaped monarch eggs, the pearly globes of the tiger swallowtail, and the gray, round, and dimpled eggs of the red-spotted purple butterfly.

The developing embryo uses all the food inside its shell. As the caterpillar matures, the egg darkens and becomes almost clear. The caterpillar is ready to hatch.

Hungry Caterpillars

The tiny caterpillar's jaws cut an opening in the eggshell for the head to emerge first. The body wiggles and twists back and forth to free itself completely. At that point, the caterpillar turns and eats its first meal—its own eggshell. It has the nutrients that the caterpillar needs for a good start in life.

Many writers describe caterpillars as eating machines. Phil Schappert, author of *A World for Butterflies*, describes a caterpillar "as an open-ended tube with a mouth at one end, an anus at the other, and a stomach in between." The caterpillar simply must convert plant matter into animal matter, for it is the only growth stage of the butterfly cycle.

Caterpillars eat greedily. They can strip leaves bare, leaving only the veins. The young larvae look for the plant's tender new leaves, as older leaves may have a waxy coating or be tough and stringy. Not only are they harder to chew, but they are less nutritious.

Most caterpillars alternately feed and rest during the day, but some feed only at night. The long-tailed skipper curls a leaf around itself to hide by day from hungry predators. At night, it unrolls from its hiding place and begins eating.

Trading Skins

Caterpillars grow quickly. They soon outgrow their exoskeletons and must molt; that is, they shed the old skin, revealing the new one underneath. Caterpillars will molt three to five times in their lives. The time between molts is the instar period.

Molting takes a few days. The caterpillar places down a glob of silk to secure its hold. Then it forms a second skin under the old one, separating the skin by a thin layer of fluid. When it is ready to molt, the larva takes in air. The body swells so the old skin splits apart, and the caterpillar wiggles out. It rests until its head and new skin harden before it starts to move and feed again.

During each instar period, the caterpillar eats more food, grows bigger, and can easily double in size. At maturity, just before pupating, a caterpillar reaches its maximum size. It will weigh more than 3,000 times its hatching weight. In contrast, a human increases his or her weight only sixteen to twenty-five times from birth to adulthood. If people grew like caterpillars, a grownup might weigh 21,000 pounds (9,525 kg) instead of 125 to 175 pounds (57–79 kg).

A caterpillar's size at its last instar also fixes the size of the adult butterfly. If, for example, a caterpillar is unable to find enough food, it may pupate early. The result would be an adult smaller than others of the same species. Adult butterflies do not grow in size.

Avoiding Predators

Juicy caterpillars make a great meal for other insects and birds. For the caterpillar, it never ends; there is always another predator lurking nearby. To survive, caterpillars evolved different strategies to defend themselves.

The greenish color of the cabbage white and alfalfa cater-pillars matches the host plant so well that they become almost invisible. The spiny black caterpillar of the gulf fritillary has two reddish stripes on each side of its body. This coloration along with the spines help disguise its body.

There are caterpillars that change as they develop. A young tiger swallowtail looks like a bird dropping. Later, it dramatically alters its appearance to become fat and green with startling yellow and black eyespots.

When disturbed, many swallowtail caterpillars defend

THE VELVETY BLACK MOURNINGCLOAK CATERPILLARS USE THEIR SPINES AND THE ROW OF REDDISH-BROWN PATCHES ON THEIR BACKS TO DETER PREDATORS.

themselves by thrusting out a forked gland call the osmeterium. Located just behind the head, the y-shaped organ appears as an orange-forked tongue. The similarity to a snake's tongue and the unpleasant odor the gland spews out discourages many predators.

The caterpillars of monarchs and their relatives retain the poisonous toxins from the milkweeds they eat. The alternating yellow and black bands on the caterpillar's body serve as warning colors to predators. One bite is enough to convince a bird not to touch a monarch caterpillar again.

After shedding its old skin, this passion vine caterpillar begins a new search for food.

A caterpillar lives, on average, from three to four weeks. If it finds enough food and somehow escapes being eaten, it is ready for its final molt.

The Big Sleep

Usually, the caterpillar moves away from its host plant to search for a good spot to pupate. It must firmly anchor itself to the twig or object. With its head down, it spins a pad of silk and attaches it to the twig. Then it turns around and grasps the silk pad with its cremaster, or anal hook.

The caterpillar may continue to spin silk to make a supporting girdle around its body. Head up is the typical position for many butterfly pupae, such as the citrus swallowtail and the orange tip. Others hang with their heads down or pupate in the ground among the leaves.

While the chrysalis forms, the caterpillar rests. Then it wiggles vigorously, and the skin splits. The pupa emerges, and it moves the hooks of the cremaster to the silk pad. Secured, the soft pupa squirms some more until the old skin drops off.

Before the chrysalis hardens, it is vulnerable to parasites, such as the parasitic wasp. The wasp lays its eggs inside the chrysalis. Instead of a butterfly, a wasp emerges from the chrysalis.

Like the egg, the chrysalis is immobile and vulnerable to birds and other creatures that see it as tasty food. Its best hope for survival is to blend into its surroundings or change color to resemble its resting place.

As an example, the chrysalis of the owl butterfly appears as a dead leaf. In summer, the zebra swallowtail caterpillar makes its chrysalis green to match the green leaves. In fall, that same chrysalis may be brown, so it blends into the leafless landscape. The shiny yellow-green chrysalis of the queen butterfly need not

ITS SILKEN PAD SECURELY HOLDS THIS CATERPILLAR AS IT BEGINS ITS PRE-PUPA STAGE.

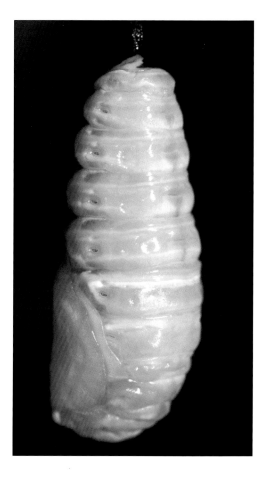

THE REFLECTIVE SURFACE OF A GREEN MONARCH CHRYSALIS ALLOWS IT TO TAKE ON THE APPEARANCE OF ITS SURROUNDINGS AND PROVIDES CAMOUFLAGE.

hide because predators soon learn it is poisonous. Unlike eggs, some pupae can twitch and quiver if disturbed, and with luck, scare off a potential predator.

A Miracle Happens

Throughout its life, the caterpillar's body contains dormant growth areas called imaginal buds. They will eventually form the organs and wings of the adult butterfly. When the caterpillar enters the pupal stage, the imaginal buds start to grow.

Inside the pupal case, the caterpillar dissolves into a thick soup. It is a chemical mix for the growth of the imaginal buds and for the rearrangement of the cells into an adult butterfly. Once the transformation is complete, the chrysalis becomes clear, so the wings, antennae, and legs are faintly visible.

Ready to emerge, the adult butterfly pumps body fluids into its head and thorax, causing the chrysalis to split. The adult pushes with its feet until it clears the pupal case and hangs free. It expels a few drops of waste fluid called meconium that had accumulated in its pupal phase.

Butterfly Life Cycle

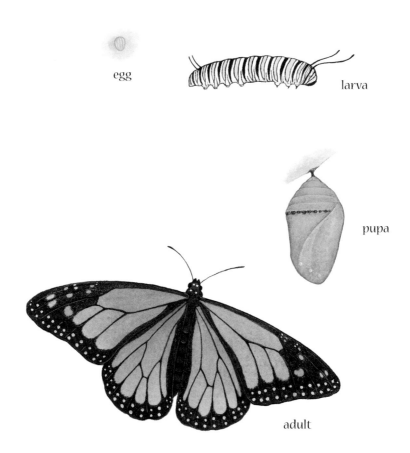

egg

larva

pupa

adult

AS ITS PUPA CASE SPLITS, THE SWALLOWTAIL STRUGGLES TO EMERGE.

Head up, the adult clutches the empty chrysalis case or a twig with the claws on its tarsi. By tightening its muscles, the butterfly moves fluid from its body into its soft, crumpled wings until they expand completely. It happens quickly, so the wings do not dry before they are fully open. The butterfly remains quiet, holding its wings apart, as they dry and harden. Then the butterfly opens and closes its wings a few times, as if testing them, before flying off to find nectar.

The butterfly has come full circle: A miraculous transformation has completed the cycle from egg, to caterpillar, to pupa, to adult.

5 Behavior

> BROWN AND FURRY CATERPILLAR IN A HURRY;
> TAKE YOUR WALK TO THE SHADY LEAF OR STALK.
> MAY NO TOAD SPY YOU, MAY THE LITTLE BIRDS PASS BY YOU;
> SPIN AND DIE, TO LIVE AGAIN A BUTTERFLY.
>
> —Poet Christina Rossetti (1830–1894)

The swallowtail butterfly moves away from its pupal case and grasps a twig with its clawed feet. Hanging upside down, the butterfly waits for its wings to harden. The warm sunny morning turns cool, and rain falls as dark clouds spread across the sky. Now the butterfly has no choice but to wait for the sun to return before it takes its maiden flight.

Butterflies glory in the sun. Being ectothermic, or cold-blooded, their body temperatures are close to their surroundings. As a butterfly raises its body temperature fifteen or twenty degrees to 77 to 110 degrees Fahrenheit (25–43° C), it becomes more active and can fly.

It does so by basking, soaking up both the sun's rays and

THE POLLEN COVERING THE BUTTERFLY'S PROBOSCIS
PROVIDES A PROTEIN-RICH MEAL FOR THE BUTTERFLY.

heat from a rock, leaf, or soil below. The butterfly spreads its wings open and turns its back to the sun. Dark-bodied and dark-scaled species, such as black swallowtails, absorb heat easily and can raise their temperature to 90° F (32° C).

A constant high air temperature is harmful to butterflies. It can reduce egg laying and shorten a butterfly's life span. To keep cool, a butterfly seeks shade and avoids flying during the hottest time of the day.

Winging It

Butterflies know instinctively how to fly and are excellent flyers. They use different flying techniques to lift off, maneuver, fly steadily, and land. Butterflies hold both wings together in flight and flap them at the same time. In contrast, dragonflies flap their two pairs of wings separately.

Heavy-bodied skippers with small pointed wings must flutter them rapidly to stay airborne. They dart about visiting flowers and do not fly too far or high. The flight of large-winged swallowtails is generally slow and gliding but can be powerful and fast if startled. The monarchs, known to migrate great distances, have large wings and slender bodies. They beat their wings slowly, alternating with long glides. Moreover, they make use of the wind to carry them. In that way, monarchs fly at speeds of 11 miles (17.7 km) an hour and can travel 80 miles (129 km) a day while migrating.

Exotic Foods

Whether flying fast or slow, butterflies spend a good part of their day seeking a sugary liquid called nectar. It is a high-energy food that powers the muscles for flight.

Other unlikely foods attract butterflies as well. They sip on the liquids of rotting fruits and vegetables. Many butterflies even feed on the juices of carrion (decaying animals), dung, or bird droppings. The more rotten and liquid an item is, the easier it is for the insect to take it in through the proboscis. Viceroys feast on the honeydew produced by aphids. Zebra longwings go one step further by making use of the pollen that collects on their proboscis and legs. With a drop of saliva, the pollen dissolves into an easy-to-digest liquid that the butterflies drink. The non-nectar food, according to entomologist Gary Noel Ross, provides protein, minerals, and salts that aid butterflies in reproduction and body health. The pollen drink may explain why longwing butterflies live several months longer than most butterflies.

Puddling

For a long time, entomologists wondered why butterflies gather around a mud puddle. Called puddling, males, in particular, stop at a mud puddle or wet spot where water regularly collects and then evaporates. Entomologists believe the concentrated salt as well as the other minerals in the puddle enrich the spermatophore the male passes to the female during mating. The minerals may also help produce male sex pheromones, which are important in courtship.

Diapause/Hibernation

After a female lays her eggs, she does not look after them or care for them. If the conditions are right, the eggs will hatch. The caterpillars will find enough food plants to eat, then grow and pupate. Often, though, change in temperature, daylight, or lack of available food leads to diapause, or hibernation, dormant resting periods.

BUTTERFLIES SWARM ON THE DAMP GROUND ALONG THE CAUABURI RIVER IN
NORTHERN AMAZONAS STATE, BRAZIL. THE PUDDLERS SUCK UP MINERAL SALTS
FROM THE MUD.

Diapause may occur in temperate climates in response to
the short, cool days of fall. This is a signal that winter is coming.
In tropical areas, diapause occurs in drier months when leaves
are too old and tough for caterpillars to chew, and nectar is

scarce. Each species has a specific stage in its life cycle when it enters a dormant resting period, so it can survive winter or other harsh conditions.

The tailed copper is one of several butterflies that enters a diapause period in the egg stage during winter. With the return of spring weather, the egg hatches and development continues. Viceroys and admirals overwinter as caterpillars. The young larva constructs its winter home from a leaf by forming it into a tube. The larva lines the tube with silk and wraps it around its body, like a blanket. More silk fastens the leaf-tube, or hibernaculum, to a twig on which it hangs all winter.

Other butterflies, as well as skippers and moths, overwinter or hibernate in the chrysalis stage. Hibernation ends as spring returns or conditions improve.

A few species brave the cold as adults by living in the inactive state of hibernation. Mourningcloaks and anglewings find shelter from the freezing weather by hiding in hollow trees, under rocks, in caves, or other dark places. Hibernation ceases when there is constant warm temperature.

Some butterflies respond to the changing seasons by heading north in the summer as tender green plants emerge or by migrating south to a warmer area in winter.

Long Journeys

The painted lady, buckeye, and red admiral, all in the Nymphalidae family, migrate northward each spring and into the summer. Their preference for weedy larval foods, such as thistles and nettles, drives their northerly journey. The butterflies do not make a round-trip, but die as the weather gets colder. The next spring new migrants will appear.

Monarchs, true migrants, escape cold winter by migrating

south. In early fall these butterflies stop mating and start to put on weight for the long trip south. Masses of monarchs travel an extraordinary 2,000 to 3,000 miles (3,200–4,800 km) on a southward journey. Monarchs east of the Rocky Mountains fly to forests high in the Mexican mountains. Monarchs west of the Rockies make their way to groves of trees along the coast of California.

The butterflies are able to survive the long trek because of fat stored in their abdomen. During their flight, the monarchs will stop to sip nectar on fall wildflowers, refueling their energy supplies just as people stop for dinner during a long trip.

In March, as the days get longer and warmer, the monarchs become more active. They mate and then start the northward journey. Most females lay their eggs on the first milkweed plants they find and die soon afterwards. About one percent of the females, though, make a complete round-trip, laying eggs along the way until they reach Canada.

The first eggs hatch, and the new generation of monarchs flies north. They live only two or three weeks, but their offspring will continue the northerly migration. By the end of summer, the fourth or fifth generations reach southern Canada, the limit for milkweed growth. In the fall the cycle repeats as these great-great grandchildren follow the migration route south to overwintering grounds.

How do these delicate creatures find their way, never having made the journey before? It has been a mystery. From new studies, scientists believe that monarchs navigate with the Sun, using both an internal compass and map. Insects can tell where the Sun is by the pattern of polarization in sunlight. Butterflies know that in the morning the Sun is in the east. To fly south, the monarch simply faces the Sun and turns right. On cloudy days, the butterfly can still navigate by seeing the patterns of scattered light created by the Sun.

Predators

At every stage of their life cycles, butterflies are food for other animals and even for a few plants. And why not? Butterfly eggs, caterpillars, pupa, and adults are plentiful and nutritious.

Garden spiders catch butterflies in their webs. Crab spiders grab them when they stop to sip nectar from flowers. Birds and lizards pick off eggs, caterpillars, and pupae from foliage. In fact, birds rely on the larvae of butterflies and other insects to

TRAPPED IN A SPIDER WEB, THIS BUTTERFLY WILL NOT ESCAPE.

A PREYING MANTIS IS A FEARSOME PREDATOR. HERE IT HAS CAUGHT A MONARCH BUTTERFLY.

feed their young. Birds also nab butterflies in flight. Flies, wasps, dragonflies, and mantids eat large numbers of caterpillars and butterflies.

They are particularly vulnerable to parasitoids, organisms that live off and kill other organisms. The Ichneumonid wasp will lay her eggs in a caterpillar or pupa. When the wasp's eggs hatch, they feed on the caterpillar or pupa and kill it. Eventually, an adult parasitic wasp appears instead of a butterfly.

The mortality (death) rate of butterflies in the immature stages is very high. Barely one or two eggs out of a hundred will ever become adults.

Defense Camouflage

How do butterflies survive in a world where so many creatures see them as a meal? Butterflies cannot defend themselves by inflicting a painful bite, or by jabbing with a piercing stinger. But they are equipped with a wondrous array of spots on their wings. With them, butterflies can disappear into their surroundings, mimic a poisonous species, a leaf, or something else. Butterflies show off their bright wing colors to warn of poison and try to fool predators in many other ways.

Imagine a bird flying through the tropical rain forest, chasing a brilliant metallic-blue morpho, when suddenly the butterfly vanishes. It lands and closes its wings, so only the brown spotted undersurface is visible, and the morpho blends easily into the dense trees. The confused bird overlooks the brown leaf and continues to search for the blue butterfly. Camouflage has worked successfully for the morpho this time. At other times, the flashing of morpho's shiny wings surprises and frightens a would-be predator long enough for the butterfly to fly away.

The Indian leaf butterfly is a truly remarkable example of

PLUMP AND GREEN, THIS EASTERN TIGER SWALLOWTAIL CATERPILLAR IS WELL CAMOU-
FLAGED. ITS BRIGHT YELLOW AND BLACK EYESPOTS HELP THE DECEPTION.

disguise. When it holds its wings upright and together, their shape and ashy brown color closely matches those of dead leaves. To complete the camouflage, a tail on its hind wing looks like a twig. The eye is fooled into thinking the butterfly is really a part of the tree.

The tropical owl butterfly has huge eyespots on the under-surface of its hind wings that look like owl eyes. Vertebrates recognize eyes as part of the butterfly's head, so the false eyes divert a would-be predator's attention away from the butterfly's vulnerable real head and body. It is better to lose part of a wing than risk being eaten altogether. Sometimes, the bold eyespots frighten birds momentarily, leaving the butterfly time to escape.

For the tiny gray hairstreak, two heads are better than one. Deceptive colors, orange or red eyespots and white-tipped tails, appear on the hind wings. With its wings closed, the eyespots

To avoid predators, this cracker butterfly perches on the trunk of a tree. The butterfly's wings perfectly resemble the patterns of the tree's bark.

look like eyes and the tails like antennae. The bold markings draw the predator's attention away from the real head. To aid in the deception, the hairstreak often rubs its hind wings together so the tails move like antennae.

Warning Colors

Butterflies have another line of defense called aposematism, or warning coloration. Bright red, orange, and yellow are typical warning colors; the same colors we use in traffic signs and emergency vehicles. The colors advertise that the butterfly is not only distasteful but poisonous as well. Predators learn that color combinations such as black and red, black and yellow, or white and black are repulsive.

To become poison-laden, the larvae feed on toxic plants. For example, the caterpillars of the tropical longwing butterflies—zebra and gulf fritillary—feed exclusively on poisonous passion vines, while the monarch and queen caterpillars eat only poisonous milkweeds. The larvae concentrate the poisonous chemicals in their bodies and pass them on to the adult's body and wings. Somehow, the chemicals do not harm the insects.

THE LARGE BOLD EYESPOTS ON BOTH THE LOWER AND UPPER WINGS SCARE PREDATORS AWAY FROM THE PEACOCK BUTTERFLY.

Birds that eat a poisonous butterfly immediately become ill and vomit. Usually once is enough, and the birds avoid any butterfly with similar colors and patterns, including edible butterflies.

Mimicry

While butterflies have a marvelous array of colors and patterns, some species imitate the unique pattern of another species, even from another family. The naturalist Henry W. Bates discovered that some edible butterflies mimic poisonous ones. The resemblance is so close it is difficult to tell them apart, and the nonpoisonous butterflies benefit from the deception. The mimicry, called Batesian mimicry, only works if the species occur together.

The striking black, orange, and yellow nonpoisonous tiger pierid, in the family Pieridae, is part of a butterfly group that mimics various poisonous species, such as Isabella in the family Nymphalidae. The Isabella butterfly—also black, orange, and yellow—feeds only on the poisonous passion vine plants. Both butterflies live in tropical Central and South America.

A second kind of mimicry is Müllerian mimicry, named for Dr. Fritz Müller, who discovered the phenomenon. In it, closely related species, such as the monarch and the queen, evolved with similar color schemes. Their caterpillars eat the same toxic milkweed plants, and both are poisonous. Once a bird eats one, it avoids the other species. Each gains protection from the other.

Life Span

Even if a butterfly manages to escape its enemies, it lives for a relatively short time. The average life span for a nonhibernating butterfly is two to six weeks. But there are notable exceptions to that rule.

After leaving its chrysalis, the tiny spring azure mates, lays eggs the next day, and dies before the end of the third day. At the other end of the curve, migrating monarchs live seven to eight months before dying on the first leg of their return trip north in the spring.

We can only marvel at the complexities of a butterfly's life and life cycle, its adaptation, and its ability to survive in a harsh world.

6

North American Species

FLY, WHITE BUTTERFLIES, OUT TO SEA,
FRAIL, PALE WINGS FOR THE WIND TO TRY,
SMALL WHITE WINGS THAT WE SCARCE CAN SEE,
FLY!

—Poet Algernon Charles Swinburne (1837–1909)

Of the 700 butterfly species in North America, many are commonly found in gardens, fields, and roadsides. The following descriptions offer a detailed look at some of North America's familiar butterflies.

THE MOURNINGCLOAK TAKES ITS NAME FROM THE DARK MOURNING COATS THAT PEOPLE WORE IN THE NINETEENTH CENTURY WHEN GRIEVING THE DEAD.

Mourningcloak *Nymphalis antiopa*

Family: Nymphalidae (brush-footed butterflies)

Habitat: open woodlands, parks, gardens, and streamside

Distribution: found in North America, south to central Mexico; common throughout Europe, and in parts of central Asia

Wingspan: 2.5–4 inches (6–10 cm)

Wing color: purple-brown with a yellow band on edges and a row of blue spots at the inner edge of the yellow border

The rich maroon-brown color of this butterfly led to the unique name of mourningcloak when people in the nineteenth century wore dark cloaks, or coats, as symbols of mourning for a dead relative or friend.

Mourningcloaks are unique. With a life span of ten to eleven months, they are probably the longest-lived butterflies in North America. As winter approaches, the adults seek protected places in which to hibernate, such as tree hollows, under loose tree bark, or in piles of stone. They will survive in any crevice that protects them from the blowing cold wind and preying birds.

When spring and warm temperatures return, the tattered butterflies leave their hibernacula and bask in the Sun. The dark colors of their wings help absorb the Sun's heat. These early butterflies feed primarily on tree sap, decayed fruit, and the nectar from the first blooming shrubs. Males perch and aggressively defend their territories as they wait for females to fly by. After mating, females lay their eggs in clusters of thirty to fifty around the branches of a willow, elm, or birch tree.

The spiny mourningcloak caterpillars stay together, lining up like a well-trained troupe of dancers as they eat greedily. The caterpillars separate before pupating. The adults from this first and only brood emerge from the chrysalis in ten to fifteen days. They feed for a short time and then aestivate, or enter a summer dormancy period. When they appear again in the fall, they feed and store fat for the winter hibernation. And the cycle repeats again.

Painted Lady *Vanessa cardui*

Family: Nymphalidae (brush-footed butterflies)
Habitat: open sunny flowered fields and gardens
Distribution: common on all continents except Australia and Antarctica
Wingspan: 2–2.5 inches (5–6 cm)
Wing color: orange and black with white spots on wingtips, four eyespots on underside of hindwings

THE VIVID PINK COLORS AND LARGE EYESPOTS MAKE THE PAINTED LADY AN ESPECIALLY APPEALING BUTTERFLY.

These brightly colored butterflies get their name from the pinkish-red patch on the underside of their forewings, a reference to the swipe of red rouge women paint on their cheeks. The butterflies have a second name, thistle butterflies, because the spiny-leaved thistle plant is a favorite food of their caterpillars. These butterflies, however, use as many as one hundred different plants as host plants, including hollyhocks, asters, cosmos, and mallows. It may explain the painted lady's success in colonizing the world.

Painted ladies are strong flyers and may migrate north for hundreds of miles each spring in search of new food plants. Some individuals fly as far as 620 miles (998 km), and, in Europe, they even manage to fly over mountaintops in their quest.

If they find abundant food, most stop and lay their eggs. In less than a month, the next generation is ready to continue the journey in North America. There may be two to three generations before the last painted ladies reach southern Canada. Although some painted ladies arrive in the north each year, major migrations of thousands occur every eight to eleven years. They find a welcome in places such as North Dakota, where thistle infests more than a million acres of land. The caterpillars strip the plants bare, helping to check the noxious weed.

Most painted ladies die as the weather turns cold. Scientists believe a small number return to the south before winter to keep the migratory habit going. Some butterflies remain in the deserts of southern Arizona and Mexico to ensure there will be butterflies next year.

Two other species share the painted lady name: *Vanessa virginiensis* (American painted lady) and *Vanessa annabella* (West Coast lady).

Eastern Tiger Swallowtail *Papilio glaucus*
Canadian Tiger Swallowtail *Papilio canadensis*
Western Swallowtail *Papilio rutulus*

Family: Papilionidae
Habitat: woodlands, along streams, gardens
Distribution: Eastern: eastern United States to Rocky Mountains; Canadian: Canada and Alaska; Western: east slope of Rockies westward

TIGER SWALLOWTAILS ARE KNOWN FOR THEIR BEAUTY, VIBRANT COLORS, AND GRACEFUL FLIGHT.

Wings: 3.5–6.5 inches (9–16.5 cm)

Wing color: yellow with black stripes, tails on hindwings

These large butterflies, with their bright yellow wings, black tiger stripes, and long tails command our attention. In early summer, they sail swiftly through our gardens. Later, they will linger, flying with slow wing beats as they glide from flower to flower. They prefer to feed from long-tubed flowers that grow four feet (1.2 m) high or more off the ground.

Eastern males are always yellow, whereas females may be yellow or all black. Eastern females also have a striking blue band on their hind wings that males do not. Black-colored females resemble or mimic poisonous pipevine swallowtails when they occur in the same region. That strategy offers the female tigers some protection from predation. Male swallowtails, on the other hand, are puddlers and often gather in large numbers at mud puddles.

Female tigers lay one egg on the leaves at the top of cottonwood, black cherry, willow, and aspen trees, and on other shrubs. The lone caterpillar has plenty of food and is less conspicuous to predators than a cluster of caterpillars would be.

Clouded Sulphur *Colias philodice*

Family: Pieridae

Habitat: fields and roadsides

Distribution: across North America

Wingspan: 2–3 inches (5–7.5 cm)

Wing color: male yellow, female yellow or greenish white, hindwings have silver spot trimmed in red

This familiar butterfly plays tricks with color. Its eggs start out white, becoming pale orange before the caterpillar emerges.

THE CLOUDED SULPHUR IS IDENTIFIED BY A SILVERY SPOT ENCLOSED WITH A CIRCLE OF RED ON ITS UNDERWING.

The green caterpillar has yellow stripes at first and then turns orange before pupating. The large, beautiful chrysalis is triangular. Sometimes its green color becomes pinkish as the adult prepares to leave. This bright yellow butterfly flies from spring to fall and has multiple broods. The alfalfa sulphur (*Colias eurytheme*) is a similar species.

Eastern Tailed Blue *Everes comyntas*
Western Tailed Blue *Everes amyntula*

Family: Lycaenidae
Habitat: gardens, meadows
Distribution: common
Wingspan: three-fourths of an inch (1.9 cm)
Wing color: males bright blue above, females are blackish
brown, one or two orange spots near tails

These common butterflies are so small they could easily disappear behind a nickel. The bright blue color of a male's wings does not come from pigment. The metallic blue results from the reflection of light on the thousands of scales covering the wings' surface. Males frequently join in a puddle club to take in salts.

The blues have an unusual relationship with ants—one in which both benefit. Ants serve as bodyguards, protecting the caterpillars against predators and parasites. In turn, the caterpillars secrete sugar and protein, called honeydew, from glands on their bodies. The honeydew is a welcome source of food for the ants. Sometimes the ants even move the caterpillars to a safer feeding spot to avoid predators. Scientists find that the more caterpillars are tended by ants, the more likely they are to survive to pupate than when ants are absent. Nevertheless, it is a

A DEW-COVERED STEM
HOLDS THE TINY EASTERN-
TAILED BLUE BUTTERFLY.

delicate relationship since both ants and butterflies are dependent on specific host plants in short-grass habitats.

Zebra Longwing *Heliconius charitonius*

Family: Nymphalidae
Habitat: tropical gardens and forests
Distribution: southern United States, Central, and South America
Wingspan: 3–3.25 inches (7.5–8 cm)
Wing color: black above with narrow yellow stripes, underwings the same but with red spots at the base

Strikingly handsome, the zebra has forewings twice as long as they are wide. Despite their appearance, zebras fly slowly with shallow wing beats through open woodlands and tropical gardens. Zebras fly alone during the day. At dusk, they meet and spend the night, huddling together in a roost. Scientists think the overnight gathering spots are a way to socialize. The newly emerged zebras will follow their elders the next day to find nectar, pollen, and female pupae.

Zebras have a unique mating behavior, as well. While still

THE BLACK AND YELLOW COLORATION OF THE ZEBRA WARNS PREDATORS THAT IT IS NOT GOOD TO EAT.

in her pupa, a female releases a scent that attracts a male. He does not wait for her to emerge from the chrysalis but breaks in and mates with her. The male leaves his pheromone scent on her in an effort to drive away other males.

Female zebras lay a few eggs on the tenderest leaves of passion vines. Their black polka-dotted spiny caterpillars eat the cyanide toxic leaves and store the poison in their bodies. Ecologist Jan Meerman states,

> *The small slow-growing passionflowers evolved defenses to ward off egg-laying female butterflies. The plants developed nectar on their leaves, which attract ants and parasitic wasps. They attack and kill the butterfly eggs and caterpillars. The female butterfly responds by laying one egg on the growing tip of the vines where there are fewer ants. The plants, in turn, stop putting out new tip growth. The female butterfly must continue to look for other vines on which to lay her eggs.*

7 Butterflies and People

For many people, observing butterflies and moths is an engrossing and often obsessive hobby. It envelops artists, writers, naturalists, and folks from all walks of life.

In Pursuit of Butterflies

For years, butterflies were abundant. Collecting them became an innocent pastime for many people.

The gifted German artist and naturalist Maria Sibylla Merian (1647–1717) collected caterpillars in order to observe them and

THE ENDANGERED KARNER BLUE BUTTERFLY NEEDS THE PINE BARREN SAND DUNES WITH THE WILD PEA PLANT, THE LUPINE, TO SURVIVE.

their metamorphosis into adults. Her studies led to the publication of her illustrated book on butterflies in 1679. At age fifty-two, she and her daughter journeyed to Suriname, South America, and undertook a scientific expedition, a rarity for women at the time. Their two years in the tropics yielded significant discoveries. Merian's writings, detailed drawings, and watercolors of butterflies and flowers inspired other naturalists, including Carolus Linnaeus, the father of taxonomy.

In another century, Englishwoman and avid lepidopterist Margaret Fountaine (1862–1940) traveled extensively around the world and amassed an important collection of 22,000 butterflies. In her diaries, she noted the abundance of butterflies everywhere. "We would go back day after day with some fifty, sixty, or even seventy specimens in my collecting box." Her butterfly collection resides in the Natural History section at Norwich Castle, England.

For Lord Walter Rothschild (1868–1937), zoologist, banker, and member of the British Parliament, collecting was a passion. As a young child, he showed a strong interest in insects and, by age eight, had a collection of butterflies. He studied zoology at Cambridge College, but throughout his busy banking and political career, he studied and collected butterflies, moths, and animals of all kinds.

Rothschild's expeditions into the Alps and North Africa were exceedingly productive. In Switzerland alone, he netted more than 5,000 Lepidoptera. He relied mostly, however, on paid collectors to search worldwide for new and unusual species. By 1936, his renowned butterfly and moth collection held two million specimens. He left it, along with other animal collections, to the Natural History Museum in London. His collections and others remain a reference for study, research, and the information for the field guides we use today.

The brilliant Russian-American writer Vladimir Nabokov (1899–1977) also had a love of nature that grew from a childhood interest into a lifelong devotion to butterflies. Although he had little formal training in zoology, he became a renowned expert on the blues, a group of small, diverse butterflies found around the globe.

After immigrating to the United States, he accepted a part-time position at the Harvard University Museum of Comparative Zoology. As a taxonomist, he carefully dissected butterflies to compare their distinctive characteristics in order to separate one species from another. It was at Harvard that he found that the beautiful Karner blue was a distinct subspecies, *Lycaeides melissa samuelis nabokov*, a discovery of which he was very proud. He said his time at Harvard was incredibly happy, but his happiest times were the butterfly-collecting trips he took every summer. In the course of his life, he published twenty-two scientific articles on butterflies.

Fame came to Nabokov with the publication of the novel *Lolita*, yet he managed to balance his life as a poet, novelist, and literary critic with that of a lepidopterist. The scale and significance of his butterfly work remained largely unknown until scientists, such as Dr. Kurt Johnson, in the 1980s and 1990s examined the legacy he left in his scientific papers. Nabokov's tiny Karner blue, now endangered, has become a major symbol of the conservation movement in the American Northeast.

Sliding into Extinction

Just forty years ago, Karner blues swarmed over the pine barren sand dunes, dense enough to form clouds. Today, they exist in small numbers in isolated pockets of habitat.

The Karner blue is not alone. The regal fritillary, a North American grassland butterfly, the large Jamaican Homerus swallowtail, and the beautiful Queen Alexandra's birdwing of Papua New Guinea are among the rare and endangered butterflies of the world. The California Xerces blue disappeared in 1941 with the destruction of its last habitat.

Butterflies are part of a healthy ecosystem and are very vulnerable to any changes in it. Problems occur when humans alter the environment by destruction, pollution, and the use of chemicals. By far, the greatest threat to butterflies and most other species is habitat loss. Humans plow, bulldoze, destroy, and damage grasslands, meadows, marshes, and forests. In their place, housing developments, farms, shopping centers, roads, and commercial centers appear. In tropical forests, logged trees give way to coffee and banana plantations, small farms, or cattle ranches. The seemingly harmless practice of mowing open fields and roadsides deprives many small butterflies of food plants.

In addition, millions of tons of pesticides are sprayed each year to control insect pests, and herbicides are sprayed to destroy weedy plants. Innocent butterflies in every stage of their life cycle die as a result. A butterfly's life is complex, and the insect is defenseless when exposed to threats created by people.

The Karner Blue

For tens of thousands of years, this butterfly could be seen in pine barren sand dunes across most of the eastern United States. Its existence revolved around lupine, a wild pea plant, and fire. The Karner blue caterpillars feed only on lupine, and the health of the pine barrens depends on occasional wildfires. The fires burned off the thick undergrowth of competing plants and made it easier for lupine to grow back.

Now habitat loss has reduced the vast acreage to isolated islands of land. Even partial destruction of habitat leaves butterflies homeless. The scattered islands may not be enough to support Karner blues for long. Volunteer groups, such as Save the Pine Bush in Albany, New York, have stepped in to protect the remaining critical habitat. With their dedication, the Karner blues have a chance for survival.

Monarchs: Long-distance Flyers

Scientists estimate there may be as many as 100 million monarchs. Despite their great number, monarchs and the multiple habitats on which they depend during their annual migration could be in trouble. Human activities, including habitat destruction and the use of pesticides and herbicides, threaten the survival of monarchs in North America.

In their southern overwintering sites, monarchs are increasingly vulnerable to human actions. The cool coastal areas of California are ideal spots for the western monarchs to roost, but the pressure to develop the coastal lands continues to threaten monarch habitat.

The eastern monarchs overwinter at eleven small roosting sites at 9,000 feet (2,800 m) in the transvolcanic mountains west of Mexico City. The butterflies gather in the center of the towering oyamel trees, protected from cold winds and frost. Logging, pollution, and a growing human population are major threats to the butterflies.

With logging, the butterflies lose roosting trees. Logging, moreover, opens up the forest canopy, or cover, letting in freezing rain and snow; that increases the chance the butterflies will freeze. In 1992 and again in 1995, five million monarchs died after a snowstorm.

The Mexican government created five forest sanctuaries, yet logging continues. Two reserves are already badly damaged.

THOUSANDS OF MONARCH BUTTERFLIES COVER TREES AND BRANCHES AT THEIR WINTER HOME IN THE TRANSVOLCANIC MOUNTAINS IN CENTRAL MEXICO.

NEAR THE EL CAMPANARIO BUTTERFLY PRESERVE IN MEXICO, THE TALL TREES HAVE
BEEN CUT DOWN TO MAKE WAY FOR SMALL FARMS.

As a result, conservationists have called for a halt to logging.
Many rural people, however, want to preserve the forests, but
they also must make a living. Logging provides income. They
also use the lumber for buildings, and they farm the cleared
forest or graze cattle on it.

The issues are complex: how to find the optimum balance
between the needs of the local people and those of the monarchs.
Economic progress for the Mexican villagers must go hand in
hand with conservation of the forests. For what happens in Mexico
directly affects the number of monarchs returning north each

spring. At the same time, habitat destruction as well as pesticide and herbicide spraying throughout the monarch's range also reduces the number of butterflies.

Conservation: Butterfly Farming

A simple but effective idea combines business with conservation. Butterfly farming gives local people a reason to protect rain forests, and it creates an income for them and their families.

Butterfly farming means raising butterflies in a greenhouse, an environment protected from predation and disease. Butterflies mate and lay eggs on host plants growing in the greenhouse. Farm workers collect the eggs, which develop to the pupal stage. Each week thousands of butterfly pupae leave the tropical forests of Central America. Some go to collectors; most go to butterfly houses in Europe and North America. Collectors are happy to get perfect specimens, rather than tattered wild butterflies collected from the forests. Conservationists are happy because butterfly farming helps stop the poaching or stealing of rare species. The butterfly farmer, in addition, releases a portion of the harvested butterflies back into the rainforest to boost the wild population.

The butterfly house exhibits, with their lush green plants and warm moist air, resemble a tropical rainforest. Within a short time, adult butterflies emerge from their pupae, pump their wings, and fly freely about the exhibit. Children and adults experience the joy of watching and sometimes holding a beauty on their outstretched hands. Butterfly exhibits, which draw 12 million people a year, open the world of nature to visiting children and adults.

Many museums and zoos feature a butterfly house during the summer, a peak time for visitors. Butterfly World in South

OYAMEL SEEDLINGS ARE GROWN ON THE ROSARIO TREE FARM IN MEXICO. WHEN
LARGE ENOUGH, THEY WILL BE PLANTED ON LOGGED LAND TO PROVIDE MONARCH
BUTTERFLY HABITAT.

Florida takes advantage of Florida's semitropical climate and setting to exhibit 5,000 butterflies yearly. Eighty species, including the blue morpho and owl butterflies, fly, feed, court, and dance in the large rainforest exhibit.

One supplier to butterfly exhibits is Green Hills Butterfly Farm in Belize, a typical butterfly farm. It is also a place where visitors get a tour of the butterfly-breeding center, learn about the butterflies of Belize, and see butterflies in all stages of their life cycle.

In 1994, ecologist Jan Meerman bought fifty acres of pasture. The forest grew back quickly in the absence of cattle, and Meerman and his wife started their butterfly farm. It is labor-intensive. The Meermans have ten Belizean farmworkers, and they are able to ship out 600 to 800 pupae by air each week.

FRAMED, THESE COLORFUL SOUTH AMERICAN BUTTERFLIES ARE SOLD ON THE STREET IN LIMA, PERU.

Most pupae go to exhibitors while enough remain to breed or to be returned to the rainforests.

Butterfly farming produces interest and awareness of butterflies and their habitats, and it generates income for the many small owners and their workers. It is a win-win situation.

Butterfly Ranching

With the largest butterflies in the world, Papua New Guinea has been a treasure trove for collectors. In the past, the rare butterflies would sell for hundreds, even thousands, of dollars. The people of the country did not profit from the sales, and the large butterflies disappeared from the forests. In the 1960s, the government formed the non-profit Insect Farming and Trading Agency. Today, the agency brings in $400,000 a year from the sale of butterflies to collectors, scientists, and artists.

In Papua New Guinea, the farmers raise butterflies by ranching, which differs from farming. The farmers grow nectar and larval food plants on abandoned land at the edge of the forest. The wild butterflies arrive, lay their eggs, and the caterpillars feast. The farmers harvest and raise the pupae and, through the agency, sell the adults as dead mounted specimens. Enough butterflies are left to restore populations in the forests. This is an important factor because Papua New Guinea suffers from excessive logging of its rainforests.

Farmers who take ranching seriously can make several thousand dollars a year, a bonanza in a country where the average annual income is $50. Because the local farmers see the butterflies coming out of the forest, they know their incomes depend on the survival of the insects and the preservation of the forests. The Papua New Guinea program is a small success story for conservation.

AT THE BUTTERFLY FARM OWNED BY JORIS BRINKERHOFF IN COSTA RICA, A WORKER COUNTS PUPAE.

Gardening for Conservation

The previous examples of butterfly conservation are encouraging, yet butterfly populations are declining worldwide.

Many people who want to help save these friendly insects are turning their backyards into butterfly-friendly gardens. They add nectar-rich flowers such as lantana and buddleia to their gardens to attract and feed adult butterflies. They encourage females to stop and lay their eggs by including larval plants, such as lupine, mallow, parsley, and passionflowers. They also keep their gardens free of pesticides and herbicides to ensure that butterflies will not be harmed by the use of poisons.

These small backyard sanctuaries can provide a healthy habitat that enriches the lives of the gardeners and the butterflies that frequent them.

Glossary

abdomen—the third part of an insect's body

adaptation—an acquired trait that helps an organism survive in its environment

aestivate—be inactive during summer dry seasons

androconia—scent glands commonly found in male butterflies that produce pheromones in courtship

antenna—one of a pair of long, thin, jointed appendages (feelers) found on the heads of insects

anus—the opening at the end of the digestive system through which all wastes leave

aposematism—warning coloration

bristle—a short, stiff hair

camouflage—use of color, pattern, and shape to blend into the surroundings to escape predation

carbon dioxide—the gas that is released by organisms during the process of respiration

chitin—the compound that is the major part of the exoskeleton of insects

chrysalis—the hard-shelled pupa of a butterfly or moth

conservationist—a person who promotes the saving of natural resources

copulate—to mate

cremaster—the hooked structure at the end of the chrysalis that attaches to the silken pad

crepuscular—active at dawn and dusk

crochet—the curved hook on a proleg of caterpillars and on the cremaster of pupae

crop—a pouch where food is held before digestion

diapause—a period of inactivity or the stopping of growth

diurnal—active during the day

diversity—great differences or variety

dorsal—the upper or back surface of an organism

ectotherm—a cold-blooded animal that cannot regulate its body temperature using its own internal heat

entomologist—a person who studies insects

epoch—a division of geologic time

esophagus—the tube through which food moves from the throat to the stomach

evolve—to change gradually

exoskeleton—rigid outer skeleton

foregut—the first part of the digestive system

ganglion—a nerve center composed of a mass of cells and fibers

genus—a biological ranking of species that share many specific traits

gizzard—a muscular structure in the digestive system where food is broken down into smaller pieces

habitat—a place where an organism makes its home

herbicide—a chemical preparation used to kill unwanted plants

hibernaculum—any place of hibernation

hibernate—to spend the winter season in an inactive state

hindgut—the last segment of the digestive system

host plant—the plant on which a female lays her eggs and that provides food for the caterpillars

imaginal buds—regions of uniform cells from which arise the form of an adult

immortality—living forever

instar—the period between molts of an insect

iridescent—colored with a rainbow effect

kachina—a supernatural being that plays a role in religious beliefs

larva—an immature form of an organism

lepidopterist—a person who studies butterflies and moths

lipase—a class of proteins that help digest fats

meconium—waste material from pupation

melanin—a pigment that gives the dark color to scales, skin, hair, fur, and feathers

metamorphosis—a series of changes through which an insect passes in its growth

midgut—the middle section of the digestive system

mimicry—the close resemblance of one organism to a different organism, so it benefits from the mistaken identity

molt—to shed old skin for new

myth—a traditional or legendary story

nectar—the sweet liquid formed in flowers

nocturnal—active at night

nymph—the young of an insect that undergoes incomplete metamorphosis

ocellus—a simple eye in an invertebrate

ommatidium—one of the units that make up the compound eye of insects

osmeterium—a brightly colored projecting organ that produces odor and is used in defense by Papilionid caterpillars

ostium—small opening

overwinter—to survive the winter months

oviposit—to deposit or lay eggs

parasitoid—a parasite that lives in another organism and eventually eats its host

pesticide—a chemical preparation used to kill insects and other animal pests

pheromone—a chemical substance that stimulates response by another organism

phylum—a biological ranking of organisms below kingdom and above class

pigment—a substance that gives color

proboscis—the coiled feeding tube of the lepidoptera

proleg—the fleshy abdominal leg of caterpillars

protease—a protein that helps break down other proteins in digestion

pterin—a pigment that creates orange, yellow, and red

pupa—the intermediate stage between larva and adult

roost—a perch on which animals rest

savanna—a grassland with coarse grasses and scattered trees

spermatophore—a capsule holding the sperm

sphragis—a plug the male leaves in the female's abdomen to prevent her from mating again

spiracle—an opening along the abdomen through which air enters and leaves the insect's body

subtropical—a region between tropical and temperate

tarsus—the farthest part, or foot, of an insect's leg

temperate—not too hot and not too cold

thorax—the part of the body between the head and abdomen of an insect

trachea—an internal tube that allows air to spread into the insect's body and tissues

ventral—the underside of a butterfly's wing

Species Checklist

All plants and animals have scientific names, which are written in Latin and are italicized.

A scientific name begins with the genus, or first name, and is always capitalized. It is followed by the species and subspecies, which are written in lowercase.

Some plant and animal species also have common names. They are written in lowercase unless the name comes from a proper noun. The scientific and common names of the butterflies mentioned in this book are listed below:

Superfamily Papilionoidea: true clubbed-antennae butterflies

Family Papilionidae: swallowtails

African giant swallowtail	*Papilio antimachus*
black swallowtail	*Papilio polyxines*
Canadian tiger swallowtail	*Papilio canadensis*
citrus swallowtail	*Papilio demodocus*
eastern tiger swallowtail	*Papilio glaucus*
giant swallowtail	*Papilio cresphontes*
Jamaican Homerus swallowtail	*Papilio homerus*
Old World swallowtail	*Papilio machaon*
parnassian butterfly	*Parnassius clodius*
Queen Alexandra's birdwing	*Ornithoptera alexandrae*
western tiger swallowtail	*Papilio rutulus*
zebra swallowtail	*Eurytides marcellus*

Family Pieridae: whites, sulphurs, orange tips

alfalfa sulphur butterfly	*Colias eurytheme*
brimstone or yellow brimstone butterfly	*Gonepteryx rhamni*
cabbage white butterfly	*Pieris rapae*
clouded sulphur butterfly	*Colias philodice*
orange tip butterfly	*Anthocharis cardamines*
tiger pierid butterfly	*Dismorphia amphione*

Family Lycaenidae: gossamer wings

common blue butterfly	*Polyommatus icarus*
eastern tailed blue butterfly	*Everes comyntas*
gray hairstreak butterfly	*Strymon melinus*
Hewitson's blue hairstreak butterfly	*Thecla coronata*
Karner blue butterfly	*Lycaeides melissa samuelis nabokov*

spring azure butterfly	*Celastrina argiolus*
tailed copper butterfly	*Lycaena arota*
western pygmy blue butterfly	*Brephidium exile*
western tailed blue butterfly	*Everes amyntula*
Xerces blue butterfly	*Glaucopcyche xerces*

Family Nymphalidae: brushfoots

American painted lady butterfly	*Vanessa virginiensis*
blue morpho butterfly	*Morpho menelaus*
buckeye butterfly	*Junonia coenia*
comma butterfly	*Polygonia comma*
common morpho butterfly	*Morpho peleides*
Esmeralda butterfly	*Cithaerias esmeralda*
Gillette checkerspot butterfly	*Euphydryas gillettie*
gulf fritillary butterfly	*Agraulis vanillae*
Indian leaf butterfly	*Kallima inachus*
Isabella butterfly	*Eucides Isabella*
Milbert's tortoise shell butterfly	*Nymphalis milberti*
monarch butterfly	*Danaus plexippus*
mourningcloak butterfly	*Nymphalis antiopa*
owl butterfly	*Caligo idomeneus*
painted lady butterfly	*Vanessa cardui*
postman butterfly	*Heliconius melpomene*
queen butterfly	*Danaus gilippus*
question mark butterfly	*Polygonia interrogationis*
red admiral butterfly	*Vanessa atalanta*
red-spotted purple butterfly	*Limenitis arthemis*
regal fritillary	*Speyeria idalia*
West Coast lady butterfly	*Vanessa annabella*
zebra butterfly	*Heliconius charithonia*
zebra longwing butterfly	*Heliconius charitonius*

Superfamily Hesperioidea: antennae with hooked ends-skippers

Family Hesperiidae: skippers

checkered skipper	*Pyragus communia*
fiery skipper	*Hylephila phyleus*
long-tailed skipper	*Urbanas proteus*

Additional Moth Species

Family Saturniidae: emperor moths

obsidian butterfly	*Rothscildia orizaba*

Family Tineidae: small moths

clothes moth	*Tineola bisselliella*

Further Research

If you want to learn more about butterflies, here are some books, videos, and Web sites that will help you.

Books for Young People

Brock, Jim P., and Kenn Kaufman. *Butterflies of North America*. New York: Houghton Mifflin Company, 2003.

Green, Jen. *Endangered: Butterflies*. New York: Marshall Cavendish, 1999.

Lasky, Kathryn. *Monarchs*. San Diego: Harcourt Brace & Company, 1993.

Mikula, Rick. *The Family Butterfly Book*. Vermont: Storey Books, 2000.

Ross, Gary Noel. *Everything You Ever Wanted to Know about Butterflies*. Baton Rouge, LA: Gary Noel Ross, 1995.

Stokes, Donald, and Lillian and Ernest Williams. *Stokes Butterfly Book*. New York: Little Brown and Company, 1991.

Waldbauer, Gilbert. *The Handy Bug Answer Book*. New York: Visible Ink Press, 1998.

Whalley, Paul. *Eyewitness Books: Butterfly and Moth*. New York: Dorling Kindersley, Ltd., 1988.

Zoobooks: Butterflies. San Diego: Wildlife Education, Ltd., 1995.

Videos

Audubon Society's Butterfly Gardening. 1996, Master Vision.

Butterfly and Moth. 1996, BBC Eyewitness Video.

Migration for Nature. 1999, Partridge Films.

Wild America: The Beauty of Butterflies. 1995, Marty Stouffers Films.

Web Sites

There are many Web sites with information about butterflies, many of which include links to other sites. Here are just a few.

http://alpha.furman.edu/~snyder/snyder/lep/hist.htm
The history and scope of the Lepidopterists' Society.

http://www.amnh.org/exhibitions/butterflies/
>   Site of American Museum of Natural History has answers to frequently asked question about butterflies.

http://www.butterflyhouse.org
>   Sachs Butterfly House and Education Center in Missouri is open year-round.

http://www.chebucto.ns.ca/Environment/NHR/lepidoptera.html
>   This site offers both information about butterflies and moths, as well links to other sources on Lepidoptera.

http://www.insects.org/index.html
>   This site aims to help you to really see insects for the miniature marvels they represent and to understand how intertwined our cultures have become.

http://www.monarchwatch.org
>   An educational outreach program with details about the migration of monarch butterflies in North America.

http://www.naba.org
>   The Web site of the North American Butterfly Association.

http://www.thebutterflysite.com/biology.shtml
>   Explore twelve butterfly topics with pages packed full of butterfly information.

A Few of the Organizations That Support Invertebrate Conservation

Entomological Society of America
9301 Annapolis Road, Suite 300
Lanham, MD 20706-3115
(301) 731-4535
http://www.entsoc.org

National Wildlife Federation
11100 Wildlife Center Drive
Reston, VA 20190-5362
(800) 822-6000
http://www.nwf.org

North American Butterfly Association
4 Delaware Road
Morristown, NJ 07960
(973) 285-0907
http://www.naba.org

Sonoran Arthropod Studies Institute
PO Box 5624
Tucson, AZ 85703-0624
(520) 883-3945
http://www.sasionline.org

The Xerces Society
4828 SE Hawthorne Boulevard
Portland, OR 97215
(503) 232-6639
http://www.xerces.org

Bibliography

These books were some of the material used by the author while researching this book. They offer more detailed information on an adult level.

Brewer, Jo. *Wings in the Meadow*. Boston: Houghton Mifflin Company, 1967.

Carter, David. *Smithsonian Handbooks: Butterflies and Moths*. New York: Dorling Kindersley, Inc., 2002.

Cater, W. F. *Margaret Fountaine, Love Among the Butterflies*. Boston: Little, Brown and Company, 1980.

Feltwell, John. *The Natural History of Butterflies*. New York: Facts on File Publications, 1986.

Glassberg, J. *Butterflies through Binoculars: East*. New York: Oxford University Press, 1999.

———. *Butterflies through Binoculars: West*. New York: Oxford University Press, 2001.

Johnson, Kurt, and Steven Coates. *Nabokov's Blues*. Cambridge, MA: Zoland Books, Inc., 1999.

Klots, Alexander B. *The World of Butterflies and Moths*. New York: McGraw-Hill Book Company, Inc., 1960.

Manos-Jones, Maraleen. *The Spirit of Butterflies: Myth, Magic, and Art*. New York: Harry N. Abrams, Inc., 2000.

Preston-Mafham, Rod and Ken. *Butterflies of the World*. New York: Facts on File, 1988.

Putnam, Patti and Milt. *North America's Favorite Butterflies*. Minocqua, WI: Willow Creek Press, 1997.

Schappert, Phil. *A World for Butterflies*. Toronto: Key Porter Books Limited, 2000.

Shepherd, Matthew, et al. *Pollinator Conservation Handbook*. Portland, OR: The Xerces Society, 2003.

The Xerces Society. *Butterfly Gardening*. San Francisco: Sierra Club Books, 1990.

Page numbers in **boldface** are illustrations and tables.

About the Author

GLORIA G. SCHLAEPFER shares her respect for the natural world through her writing and photography, and as a naturalist with Audubon's school tours at the San Joaquin Wildlife Sanctuary in California. She has most recently written *Cheetahs* and *Elephants* for Benchmark Books' AnimalWays series. She has also coauthored three books for children: *The African Rhinos*, *The Coyote*, and *Pythons and Boas*. Schlaepfer, who lives in Fullerton, California, has four children and four grandchildren.